HOW YOUR GOVERNMENT SPENDS YOUR MONEY

2012 Edition

I0436178

by

Robert N. Hager, Ph.D.

Booklet Proceeds

Proceed from sales of this booklet will go to Wholeschool.org, a non-profit educational organization that provides afterschool programming for young children in self-awareness. This QR Code below brings you to a video about Wholeschool.

Disclaimer

This booklet is designed to provide information about the subject matter covered. Every effort has been made to make this booklet as complete and accurate as possible. However, there may be errors both typographical and in content. Therefore, this text should be used only as a general guide and not as the ultimate source of federal income and spending information.

The purpose of this booklet is to educate and entertain. The author and Wholeschool, the non-profit to whom proceeds are going, shall have neither liability nor responsibility to any person or entity with respect to any loss or damage caused or alleged to be caused directly or indirectly by the information contained in this book.

Table of Contents

Foreword

The purpose of this booklet is to provide you with useful information about how our government spends our money. It is non-partisan. It is an objective observation of what is so with regard to income and outgo of money within our country.

The budget of the United States is really no more difficult to understand than your home budget. If you understand where the money comes from and where it goes, you have the power to suggest changes if you so desire. We elect our Congress and President, and it is our responsibility to explain to them exactly where we choose to invest our money. We pay their salaries. They are representatives of us and should act in our best interest. However, if they do not know our interests, they will act in their own best interest.

As an aerospace engineer in the 1970s, I totally enjoyed our nation's commitment to space exploration. However, after reaching the Moon, our funding for NASA began to decline and by the early 1980s I was beginning to become concerned. I contacted my Congressman and Senators for an easy explanation of the federal budget process and was told I could order the budget documents from the US Government Printing Office, which I did. A few weeks later three large books arrived each several inches thick. I attempted to read the material which turned out to be a great cure for insomnia.

I continued to struggle with the question, "Where is my tax money going and do I have any say in the matter?" I wanted to see more spending for NASA but I knew very little about all of the other agency spending and how spending for NASA compared with their budgets. So, in 1990, I took six months off from engineering to attempt to learn about the federal budget process. I again ordered the latest set of budget documents from the US Government Printing Office and, with the help of coffee, pressed on. I began to learn the budget process and see a way to present information graphically, to help me understand where the money comes from and where the money goes. I then self-published the first edition of this booklet let in 1991. Two editions followed in 1995 and 2005.

We now have the internet and the information that was in print form from the US Government Printing Office is available online. It is easy to create graphs and charts from downloadable tables of data and this e-Booklet is an example of how far technology has taken the publishing industry. Times have changed. However, the budget process has not. As a nation, we are spending more each year per person yet we, the funders, know very little about where our money is going.

It is clear that our government is ours; that we fund it with our money. It is also clear that we need the employees of our government to perform certain actions and activities that we, as individuals, cannot do or prefer not to do. However, we must be willing to tell our government how to spend our money. In order to do that, we must devote a bit of time to learn about our government and where our money has been spent in the past. That is what this booklet can do for you.

Thank you for investigation this subject with me. I believe that with understanding comes committed action. You can promote the areas where you would like to spend your tax money and I will do the same. Together, we will shape the future of our country and our priorities for ourselves, our children and grandchildren.

Bob Hager

May 24, 2012

CHAPTER ONE -- An Overview

The Federal Budget Process

The Federal Budget is determined by the President and Congress. Generally, the President submits a budget in January or February that will go into effect the coming October 1. The financial or fiscal year of the United States starts on October 1 and ends on September 30 of the next year. The date for the fiscal year is the year when the fiscal year ends.

The President's budget goes to both houses of Congress, the Senate and the House of Representatives. It is analyzed by numerous committees and additions and changes are made. Final spending and revenue bills must be agreed upon by both houses of Congress and by the President before the revised budget becomes the official spending plan for the next fiscal year.

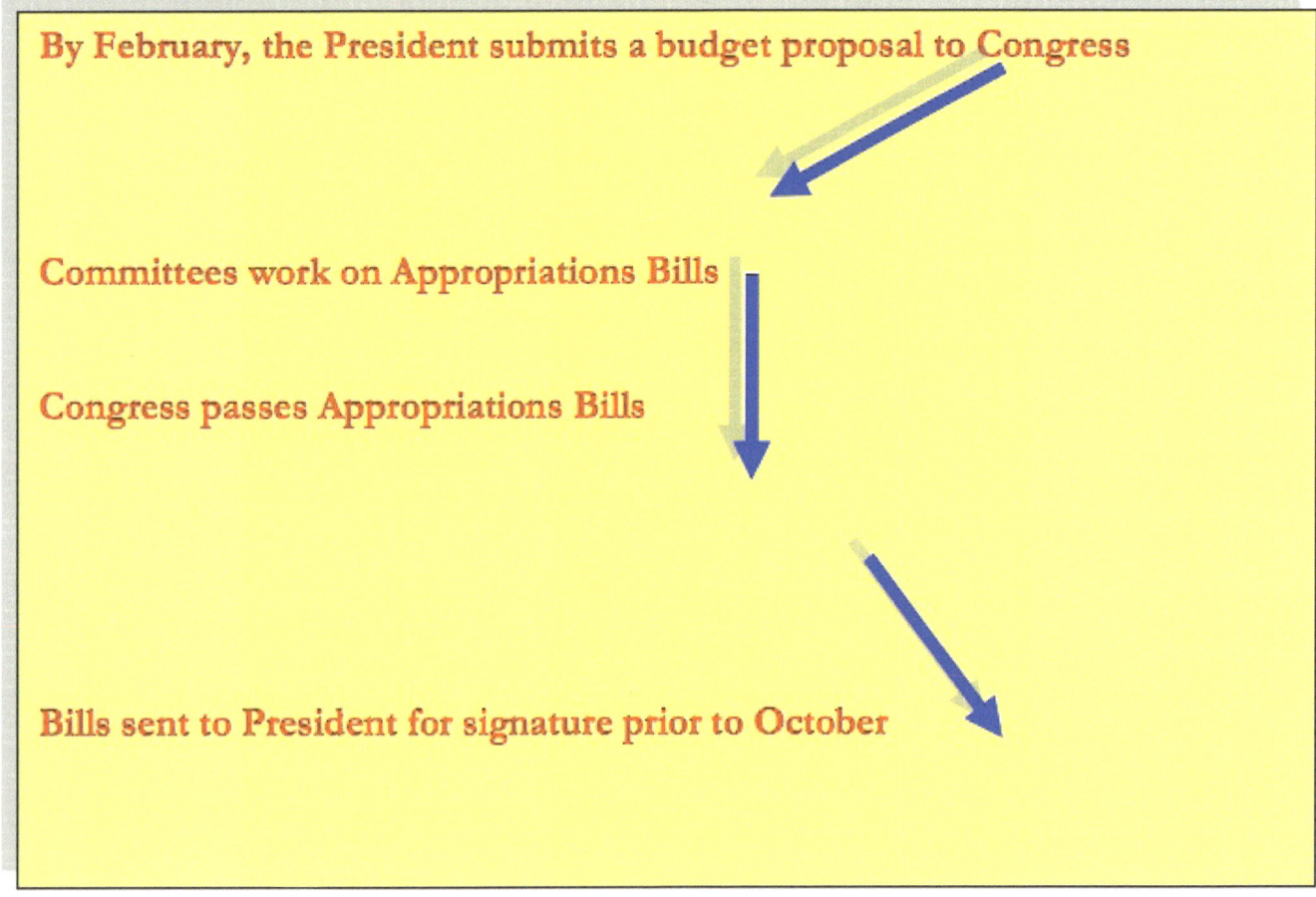

By February, the President submits a budget proposal to Congress

Committees work on Appropriations Bills

Congress passes Appropriations Bills

Bills sent to President for signature prior to October

Congress must pass--and the President must sign--13 spending bills, based upon the final budget, that detail "**discretionary spending**" in 13 general categories. These categories are similar to your home discretionary spending—they are needed, but the timing and amounts can be varied depending upon how much money is available. Entertainment spending, clothing or money spent on a vacation are examples of discretionary spending at home.

There are certain "**mandatory spending**" categories, such as interest on the public debt and Medicare and Medicaid payments that continue year after year, unless the President and Congress change the governing laws. In your household budget, mandatory spending would be the minimum payment on a credit card or a mortgage payment.

"**Entitlements**" are mandatory payments to individuals who meet some criteria of eligibility such as age or income that entitles those individuals to receive the payments.

So what happens if this procedure does not work and a budget is not approved? This has occurred before, the latest in FY 2011 and 2012. A "**Continuing Resolution**" is required. The United States Senate website gives this definition:

"Continuing resolution/continuing appropriations - Legislation in the form of a joint resolution enacted by Congress, when the new fiscal year is about to begin or has begun, to provide budget authority for Federal agencies and programs to continue in operation until the regular appropriations acts are enacted."

The US Senate Committee on Appropriations released a summary of the Continuing Resolution (CR) for 2011 containing the following statement:

"Under the CR, funding would continue at FY 2010 enacted levels for most programs. In total, the CR would provide funding at a rate approximately $1.16 billion over the FY 2010 level."

What You Will Learn From This Book

You are going to learn some amazing and surprising information about where your government spends your money. You will be able to push through the confusing words often used when talking about the budget and get to the facts. The facts are there, and they are not confusing.

For example, you will learn that the "**Social Security Trust Fund**" is neither a fund nor a trust in the normally accepted definition of the words. We are often led to believe that our Social Security payroll tax money has been invested in trust and there is some asset that will be used to finance our retirement. However, the Congressional Report on Social Security, dated August 11, 2005 states in the summary:

"The Social Security program is financed primarily through taxes, which are deposited in the U.S. Treasury and credited to the Social Security trust fund. Any revenues credited to the trust fund in excess of the costs (benefit payments and administrative costs) are invested in special U.S. obligations (debt instruments of the U.S. Government)."

Some of our payroll tax money is used to make payments to retirees each year. The excess has been borrowed by the federal government and spent on other programs. It is reported as being in a "Trust Fund" with a 2.6 trillion dollar balance. In fact, this money has been borrowed and spent with a promise to be repaid with interest by the federal government.

It is difficult to conceive of 2.6 trillion dollars. Here are some comparisons:

- *2.6 trillion dollars is 2,600 billion dollars which is 2,600,000 million dollars which is 2,600,000,000,000 dollars.*

- *2.6 trillion dollars was more than the entire federal spending for fiscal year 2005.*

- *If you split 2.6 trillion dollars with all the people 65 years old and older in the US, each would receive $65,000.*

You will also learn that the federal government spending per person more than doubled over the past 40 years and that takes inflation into account! It is worth asking whether we are receiving twice the quantity or quality of service by the federal government now, then we did in 1971.

The figure below shows the history of federal spending when both the population growth and inflation are taken into account. Spending over a 40-year period is shown in "constant dollars per person". Showing "dollars per person" being served removes changes due to population growth. Using "constant dollars" is a way to remove the changes due to inflation.

All data used to create this graph and all other graphs within this booklet were obtained from government sources. For example, total spending per year was obtained from the Budget of the United States Government: Historical Tables Fiscal Year 2012.

The yearly population data was obtained from Statistical Abstract of the United States-Population.

Federal Spending Per Person

in Constant Dollars

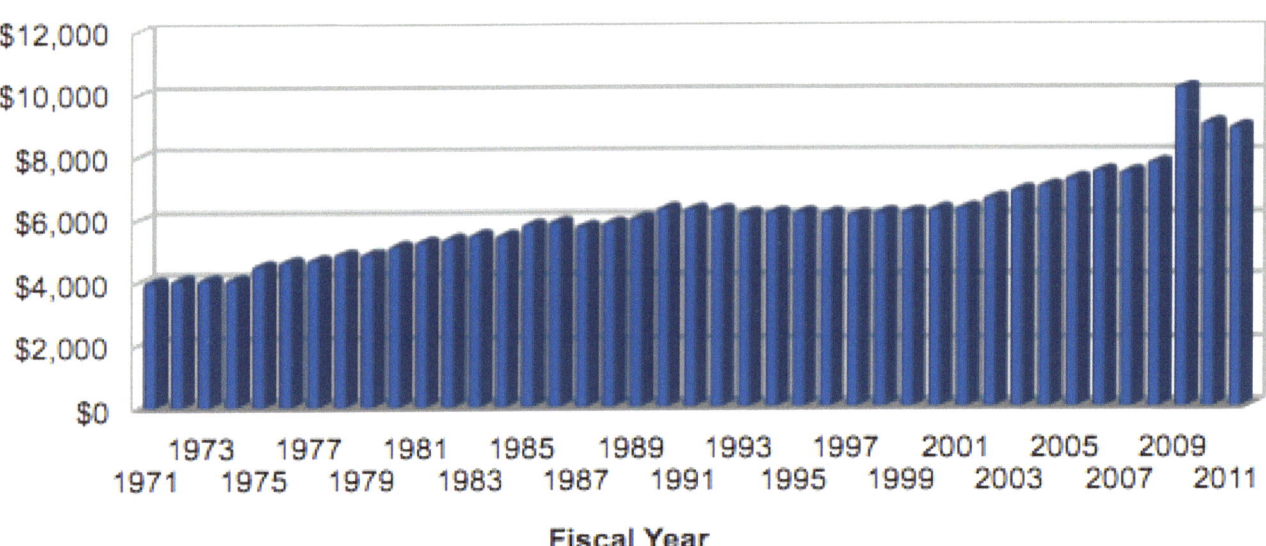

Fiscal Year

Chapter Two explains the income and outlays of the federal government for FY (Fiscal Year) 2011. This section also explains government trust funds, the dictionary and government definitions and lists data for the largest trust funds.

Social Security, the largest government trust fund, and Medicare, the third-largest fund are then discussed in some detail in Chapter Three. Graphs show the growth of these two funds over the past forty years.

Chapter Three also discusses deficit spending, with a graph showing the history of the budget surplus and deficit over the past forty years. National debt information follows, which distinguishes public debt and government debt. The histories of both are presented in graphical form.

Chapter Four of this booklet gives spending histories for various government functions over the past 40 years. Spending data is from federal historical tables for Outlays by "Function". Functions are classifications of spending that relate to similar areas. Examples of Functions are National Defense, International Affairs and Health. Spending in 2011 is detailed in this section by showing specific spending within each Function.

The historical spending graph is shown as the percent of total spending for that year. By showing spending in this manner, one can get a sense of priorities that we have as a nation and how they vary with time.

The last chapter gives information about our Congress, their average time in office, salaries and the average amount of money they raise to be elected. Since Congress has become more and more dysfunctional at our expense, we seem to be the only hope to solve the problems that this booklet brings to light. Several ideas are offered, including a link to the Simpson-Bowles "The Moment of Truth", a 65 page document offered by the Presidential Commission to bring the deficit spending of Congress to an end.

CHAPTER TWO – Here, There and Nowhere—Receipts, Outlays and Trust Funds

Where the Money Comes From

Funding for the federal budget comes from the citizens of the country. We pay individual federal income taxes. Our corporations and the companies where we work pay federal taxes on profits, which are passed back to us in added product and services costs. We also have payroll deductions for Social Security and Medicare, as do our employers. We pay other taxes on goods and services, called excise taxes, for such things as fuel for cars, trucks and airplanes, telephone usage, alcohol, tobacco, and specialty items such as jewelry.

Tax freedom day is calculated each year as the day when Americans have made enough money to pay all their federal, state and local taxes, estimated to be 29.2 percent of income. In 2012, this day fell on April 17, the same day income taxes were due.

Only those portions of our Social Security payroll taxes that are used to pay present Social Security recipients are considered "On Budget". Any amounts of these taxes received above that needed to pay present recipients are considered "Off Budget" and are not counted as part of the budget income. However, this money is required by law to be invested in government securities—that is, the government borrows this money and it is placed into the general fund and spent. The government securities are IOUs or promises to repay the money for Social Security expenses sometime in the future.

Personal Income Tax receipts are the largest contribution to fund the federal budget. In 2011, personal income tax contributed 956 billion dollars or 59% of the total "On Budget" receipts. The "On Budget" payroll taxes for Social Security contributed the next highest with 247 billion dollars or 15%. Corporate income taxes contributed 198 billion dollars or 12% of the total.

Excise taxes in 2011 amounted to income of 74 billion dollars. Highway and Airway fees and taxes contributed the most, followed by alcohol, tobacco and telephone taxes.

Finally, "Other Income" totaling 138 billion dollars consisted mostly of federal reserve system earnings, custom duty fees and estate and gift taxes, in that order. Below is a pie graph showing the "On Budget" sources of income for 2011 as segments of the whole. The total On Budget income was $1,614,278,000,000 or $1,614 billion dollars.

FY 2011 Receipts

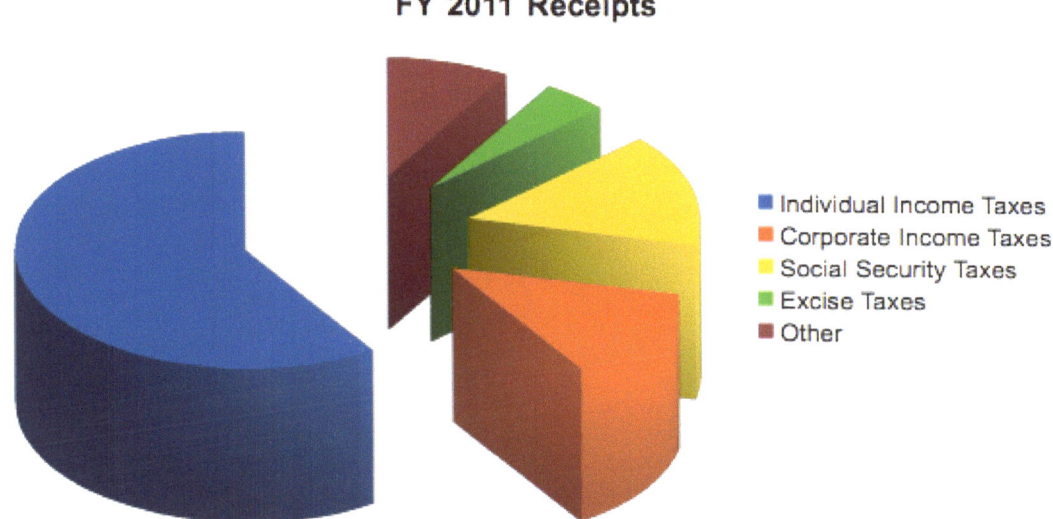

- Individual Income Taxes
- Corporate Income Taxes
- Social Security Taxes
- Excise Taxes
- Other

Where the Money Goes

Federal spending can be categorized in several ways, and a variety of terms are used to do this.

One example, that we have discussed previously, uses the terms **mandatory spending** and **discretionary spending,** dividing spending into two main areas. Mandatory spending consists of payments required by law such as interest payments on the public debt and payment to hospitals that are covered by Medicare insurance. Discretionary spending are payments made at the discretion of Congress. Money used for medical research, education, environmental protection, space flight and national defense are all discretionary spending.

Here is what the Congressional Budget Office reported for discretionary spending in 2011.

"Discretionary outlays—the part of federal spending that lawmakers generally control through annual appropriation acts—totaled about $1.35 trillion in 2011, or close to 40 percent of federal outlays. Slightly more than half of that spending was for defense. The remainder went for a wide variety of government programs and activities, with the largest amounts spent for education, training, employment, and social services; transportation; income security (mostly housing and nutrition assistance); veterans' benefits (primarily for health care); health-related research and public health; international affairs; and the administration of justice."

Mandatory spending then accounted for sixty percent of the federal budget in 2011.

Federal Spending is also be categorized by terms such as "**Superfunction", "Function"** and "**Subfunction".** Superfunctions divide spending into five broad, similar areas: National Defense, Human Resources, Physical Resources, Net Interest and Other. Functions divide each Superfunction and Subfunctions divide up Functions in even more detail.

We will be talking about Function spending in this booklet with a look at spending within eighteen discrete Functions. In Chapter Four, we will see the historical trends in the major Functions over the past forty years and provide spending information on Subfunctions under each Function for FY 2011.

Explanations of the major eighteen Functions are given below, taken from the House of Representatives Committee on the Budget website. <u>They are listed from largest to smallest outlays in FY 2011.</u>

National Defense includes the military activities of the Department of Defense, the nuclear-weapons related activities of the Department of Energy and the National Nuclear Security Administration.

Income Security consists of a range of income security programs that provide cash or near-cash assistance (e.g., housing, nutrition, and energy assistance) to low-income persons, and benefits to certain retirees, persons with disabilities, and the unemployed. Housing assistance programs account for the largest share of discretionary funding in this function.

Medicare includes only the Medicare program, which provides health insurance to senior citizens and persons with disabilities. Congress provides an annual appropriation for the costs of administering and monitoring the Medicare program. Nearly 99 percent of spending in this function occurs on the mandatory side of the budget, and almost all of the mandatory spending consists of payments for Medicare benefits.

Health includes most direct health care services programs. Some of the agencies funded in this function include the National Institutes of Health, Centers for Disease Control and Prevention, Health Resources and Services Administration, and the Food and Drug Administration. The major mandatory programs in this function are Medicaid, the State Children's Health Insurance Program, federal retirees' health benefits, and health care for Medicare-eligible military retirees.

Net Interest consists primarily of the interest paid by the federal government to private and foreign government holders of U.S. Treasury securities.

Veterans Benefits and Services covers the programs of the Department of Veterans Affairs (VA), including veterans' medical care, compensation and pensions, education and rehabilitation benefits, and housing programs. Almost 90 percent of appropriated funding goes to veterans' health care.

Social Security consists of the two payroll tax-financed programs that are collectively known as Social Security: Old-Age and Survivors Insurance and Disability Insurance (OASDI). This function includes Social Security benefit payments and funds to administer the program.

Education, Training, Employment and Social Services includes funding for the Department of Education, social services programs within the Department of Health and Human Services, and employment and training programs within the Department of Labor.

Transportation consists mostly of the programs administered by the Department of Transportation, including programs for highways, mass transit, aviation, and maritime activities. This function also includes two components of the Department of Homeland Security: the Coast Guard and the Transportation Security Administration. In addition, this function includes research program for civilian aviation.

Administration of Justice consists of federal law enforcement programs, litigation and judicial activities, correctional operations, and state and local justice assistance. Agencies within this function include: the Federal Bureau of Investigation; the Drug Enforcement Administration; Border and Transportation Security; the Bureau of Alcohol, Tobacco, Firearms and Explosives; the United States Attorneys; legal divisions within the Department of Justice; the Legal Services Corporation; the federal Judiciary; and the Federal Bureau of Prisons.

International Affairs contains funding for all U.S. international activities, including: operating U.S. embassies and consulates throughout the world; providing military assistance to allies; aiding developing nations; dispensing economic assistance to fledgling democracies; promoting U.S. exports abroad; making U.S. payments to international organizations; and contributing to international peacekeeping efforts.

Natural Resources and Environment includes programs concerned with environmental protection and enhancement; recreation and wildlife areas; and the development and management of the nation's land, water, and mineral resources.

General Science, Space and Technology includes the National Science Foundation, programs at the National Aeronautics and Space Administration except for aviation programs, and general science programs at the Department of Energy.

General Government includes the activities of the White House and the Executive Office of the President, the legislative branch, and programs designed to carry out the legislative and administrative responsibilities of the federal government, including personnel management, fiscal operations, and property control.

Energy contains civilian energy and environmental programs in the Department of Energy.

Community and Regional Development includes federal programs to improve community economic conditions, promote rural development, and assist in federal preparations for and response to disasters. This function provides appropriated funding for the Bureau of Indian Affairs, the Federal Emergency Management Agency, and provides mandatory funding for the federal flood insurance program.

Agriculture includes farm income stabilization, agricultural research, and other services administered by the U.S. Department of Agriculture.

Commerce and Housing Credit includes mortgage credit, the Postal Service, deposit insurance, and other advancement of commerce. The mortgage credit component includes housing assistance through the Federal Housing Administration, the Federal National Mortgage Association (Fannie Mae), the Federal Home Loan Mortgage Corporation (Freddie Mac).

This function also includes funding for independent agencies such as the Securities and Exchange Commission, and the majority of the Small Business Administration.

The figure below shows spending by Function for fiscal year 2011 in order from the largest to the smallest spending.

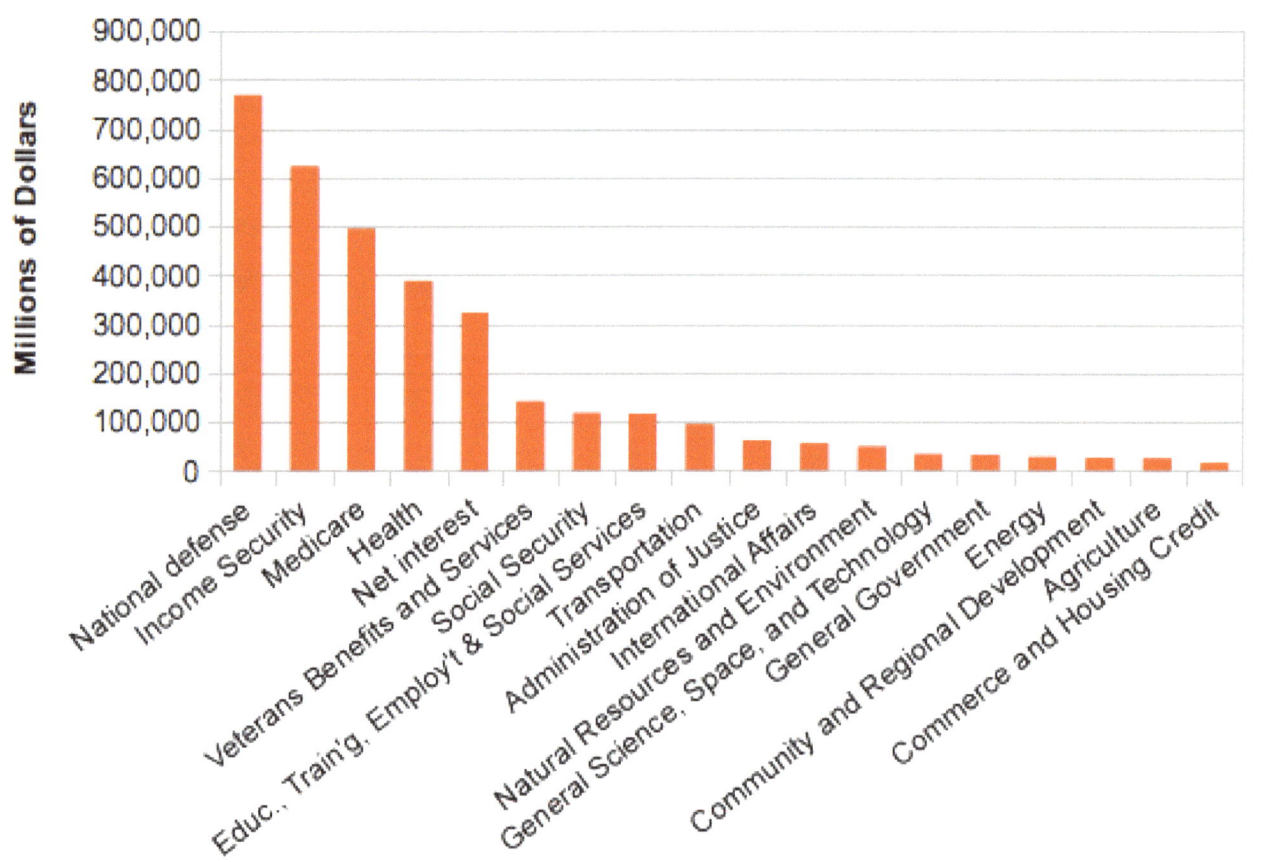

Outlays by Function

FY 2011

Total outlays for FY 2011 were 3,317,000 million dollars or 3,317 billion dollars or 3.3 trillion dollars.

Details of each Function and the subfunctions under each are given in Chapter Four, along with the historical spending as a percentage of total spending for that year. These historical graphs give an idea of the importance we, as a people, place on each category.

Now, let's take a look at Trust Funds in general. We will look in detail at the Social Security Trust Fund and the Medicare Trust fund, in Chapter Three.

Government Trust Funds

Government trust funds are accounts designated by law to keep track of receipts and outlays of money to be used for a specific purpose. The government's definition of the term "trust fund" is different from public usage. The American Heritage Dictionary defines a trust fund as "an estate, especially money and securities, held or settled in trust."

In the *Budget of the United States Government: Historical Tables Introduction Fiscal Year 2005*, the following is made:

"The term trust fund as used in Federal budget accounting is frequently misunderstood. In the private sector, "trust" refers to funds of one party held by a second party (the trustee) in a fiduciary capacity. In the Federal budget, the term "trust fund" means only that the law requires the funds be accounted for separately and used only for specified purposes and that the account in which the funds are deposited is designated as a "trust fund." A change in law may change the future receipts and the terms under which the fund's resources are spent."

In layman's terms, a trust fund is a bookkeeping account. Money from specific taxes or fees goes into the account and is used to pay for current specific expenses. Excess tax money after paying these specific current expenses must be used to purchase special federal securities or IOUs. The money paid for these IOUs is a loan to the government by the government. This money goes into the general fund account and is spent. There are no marketable assets other than federal securities contained in trust fund accounts.

There is the promise by the federal government to honor these securities by repaying the loans with interest for expenses associated with each trust account. However, the details of the repayment are determined by law, which can be modified. There is no repayment schedule and interest due is just added to the particular trust fund debt.

Here is a very simplified "at home" example of this type of trust fund.

Suppose two parents had a daughter and, when she was ten years old, they decided to put money away for her college education. So, each month they put $500 into a safe deposit box in the bank. However, each month they see something extra they wish to buy so they remove the $500 and replace it with an IOU promising to repay it with 5% interest. When their daughter reaches 18, she is ready to go to college. The parents remove the safe deposit box with 96 IOUs, each for $500. They owe themselves $48,000 plus interest.

The IOUs do not make it any easier to send their daughter to college. They still must figure a way to obtain more money over the next four years to pay for college expenses. As they find money and spend it on their daughter's college education, they will tear up some IOUs. It really makes no difference whether they had the IOUs in the safety deposit box or not.

Sometimes we hear government officials talk of "insolvency" of a trust fund or that we should put them in a "lock box". This makes no real sense and just leads us to believe there are marketable assets in a physical location. There are not. We, the public, will need to figure out the way to finance Social Security and Medicare and other trust account expenses by raising additional money through taxes and fees or by borrowing from the public.

The largest government trust fund is the Social Security Trust Fund followed by the Federal Civilian Employees Retirement Fund and the Medicare Trust Fund.

The total balance of all government trust funds, as of 2011, was 4,299.4 billion dollars or 4.3 trillion dollars. That total trust account balance is one trillion dollars more than total federal outlays for FY 2011.

The following table shows five of the larger trust funds, their income, outgo and balance, in millions of dollars, as of 2011.

You can see that the first three trust funds are accumulating a balance while the last four are either staying even or reducing the balance.

Trust Fund	Income	Outgo	Balance
Social Security	808.8	745.5	2644.9
Federal Employees Retirement	43.1	42.9	803.4
Military Retirement	98.2	55.3	361.5
Medicare Hospital (HI)	229.8	269.2	240.7
Medicare-Supplemental Medical Insurance	297.1	304.6	64.5
HIghway	37.8	45.0	22.0
Railroad Retirement	10.2	11.3	20.5

It is also worth noting that whenever the outgo exceeds the income and the balance is reduced, it requires that money be obtained from somewhere, usually by borrowing from the public. There is really no money in the fund; just federal IOUs.

CHAPTER THREE – Problems of Our Time

Social Security

The Social Security Act of 1935 provides a continuing income to workers age 65 after retirement. The Social Security Amendment of 1954 lowers the age to 62 and provides benefits to disabled workers aged 50 to 65.

Since 1935 until the mid 1980s, payroll taxes collected from employees and employers were maintained nearly equal with payments made to retirees. The law was changed from time to time to adjust the tax rate and the amount of a person's annual salary that was taxable as payments to individuals increased. For example, in 1936 the Social Security tax that a wage earner was 1% of the first $3,000 earned. The employer paid this same amount also. Over the years, these amounts have steadily grown until now the wage earner's tax and the employer's tax is 6.2% of the first $106,800 earned. In some years, a bit more was collected than spent and in others, a bit less.

In 1983, a bill was signed into law that made numerous changes in the Social Security and Medicare programs. The "Social Security Amendments of 1983" resulted in steady increases in the amount collected from payroll taxes over the amount spent on payments to retirees. Social Security taxes increase about 0.3 % for employed workers and about 3.0 % for self-employed workers.

Every year, retirees are paid from the *Old-Age, Survivors, and Disability Insurance (OASDI)* payroll taxes collected. The amount left over is required by law to be invested in special government securities (IOUs). There are two special accounting funds that keep track of the excess taxes that have been borrowed.

One is called the "Old Age and Survivors Insurance Fund (OASI)" and the other is the "Disability Insurance Fund (DI)". This left over money is borrowed by the government and spent on other programs. This first graph shows this sudden growth since 1987 of the OASI Fund.

The amount owed by the government to Social Security OASI exceeds 2.6 trillion dollars (2,600 billion dollars or 2,600,000 million dollars).

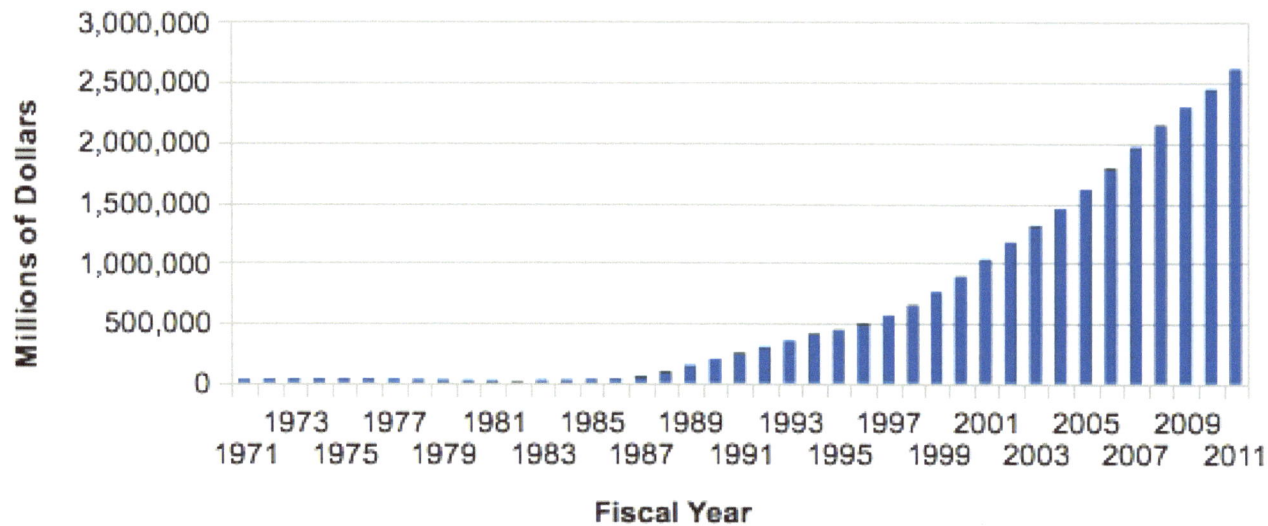

In 1994, a greater portion of total Social Security taxes went into the Disability Insurance Trust Fund of Social Security in order to avoid a shortfall in the fund in 1995.

This graph shows an increase in the fund due to this increase in taxes.

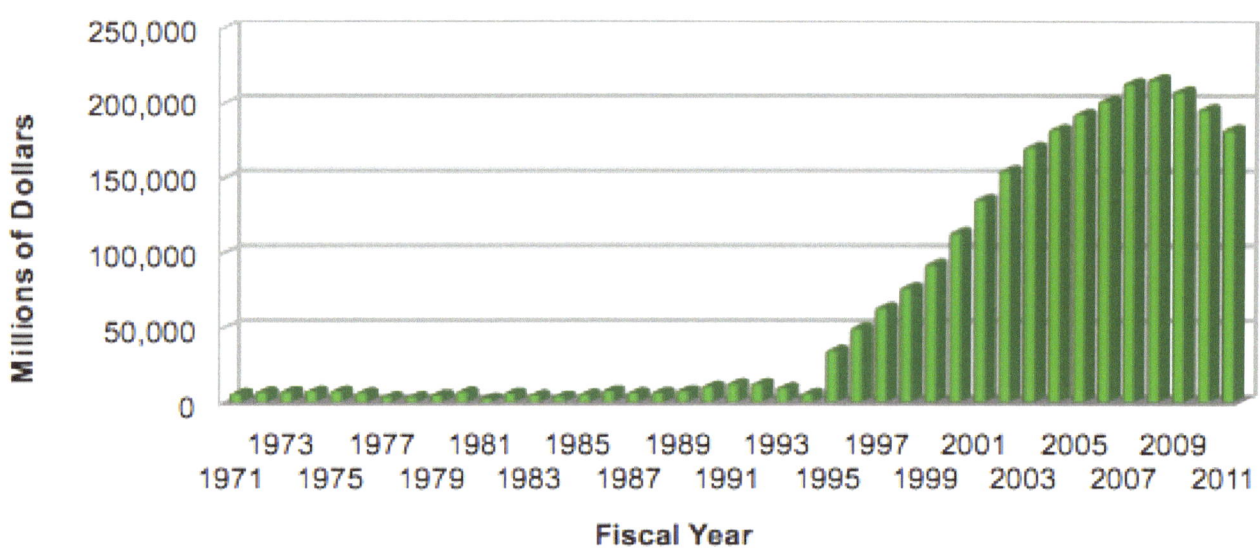

Social Security Trust Fund

Disability Insurance

In 2008, disability outgo began to be more than income and the fund shows a decrease. Any decrease in a trust fund means that money has to be found elsewhere to make the actual outgo payments, since there is no real money in the fund.

As we discussed in the preceding section, the term "Trust Fund" is misleading. The term is used to name the bookkeeping account keeping track of the amount of money owed to the federal government, by the federal government. There is no money or other marketable assets in these trust fund accounts, only government IOUs honoring the debt owed. Interest is routinely credited to these accounts which adds to the total amount owed.

According the report of the special committee on aging, United States Senate, presented on May 13, 2010, it is estimated that in 2016, if no changes are made in the payroll tax rate or the taxable income, that is, if the tax rate for employees and employers remains at 6.2 % of the first earned $106,800, the payroll tax receipts will again equal retiree payments. There will be nothing left over for the government to loan to itself for other programs. At that time, more and more of retiree payments will have to come from the government repaying these loans to Social Security or the payroll tax formulas will need to be adjusted upward again through new law.

The DI Trust fund is projected to be exhausted in 2024 and a reallocation of total taxes will have to be made as was done in 1994. If no changes are made in the tax formulas and the difference between receipts and payments is made up by the government repaying its loans and interest, Social Security OASDI is estimated to remain funded by current law through the year 2036 when both funds are reduced to zero.

Medicare

Medicare provides health insurance to people of age 65 and older, certain people with disabilities who are under 65 and people of any age who have permanent kidney failure. It provides basic protection against the cost of healthcare but it does not cover all medical expenses or the cost of most long-term care.

Because of the "Medicare Modernization Act of 2003, Medicare now has three parts: Part A Medicare, or *Hospital Insurance,* Part B Medicare or *Supplemental Medical Insurance* and Part D Medicare or *Prescription Drug Insurance*.

Medicare Part A Hospital Insurance (HI) has been financed through a payroll tax paid by all employees and employers. Part B and Part D are financed through voluntary premiums. The tax rate and limit of taxable income for Medicare Part A have been increased as expenses increase. For example, in 1967, the tax rate for employees and employers was 0.35% on the first $6,600 earned. Now, the tax rate for both is 1.45% on unlimited earnings.

Similar to Social Security, the "Social Security Amendments of 1983" resulted in steady increases in the amounts collected from payroll taxes over the amount spent on payments to Hospital Insurance. This tax, like the Social Security payroll tax, is credited to a bookkeeping account called the **Medicare Hospital Insurance Trust Fund**.

Expenses are debited from this account. Excess payroll tax money, above HI expenses, must be used to purchase special government interest-bearing securities (IOUs). This excess money then goes to the general fund to be spent on other programs. The following graph shows the growth of the money owed to Medicare by the federal government.

Medicare Trust Fund

Hospital Insurance

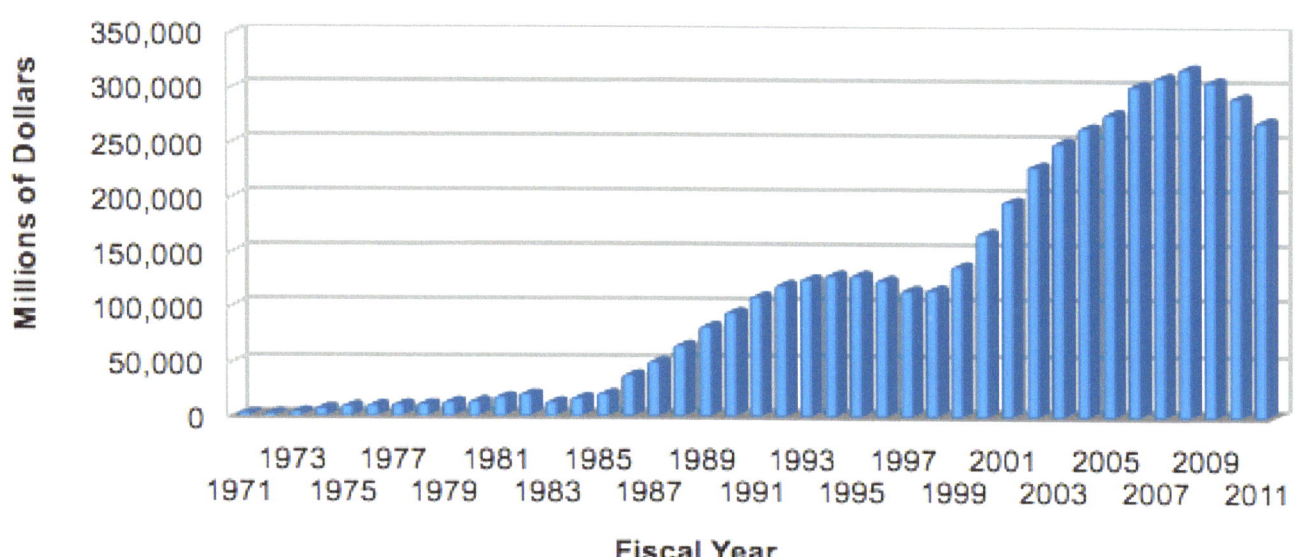

Fiscal Year

Beginning in 2009, payroll tax income was not sufficient to cover all HI expenses, and it was necessary for the federal government to actually pay some owed interest money into the Medicare Trust Fund account. From now on, under present law, more and more money to pay HI expenses will have to come from the government, reducing the debt and interest owed the Medicare Trust Fund account. However, new law can change the payroll tax formula at any time to increase the Medicare payroll tax. If no changes are made in the HI payroll tax law, the Medicare Trust Fund account is projected to reach zero by the year 2024.

Medicare Part B is funded through a monthly premium from individuals over sixty-five years old who request Part B coverage. There is also an annual deductible amount which must be met before beginning payments for allowable medical expenses. This premium and deductible have been adjusted upward since the creation of Medicare in 1967. For example, the premium was $3 per month, with a $50 deductible in 1967. Many increases have occurred since 1967 and in 2006, the premium was increased to $88.50 per month with a deductible of $124.

Because of new law provided in the Medicare Modernization Act of 2003, Medicare Part D for prescription drug coverage is also funded entirely through voluntary premiums. Both Part B and Part D programs are designed to forecast increase costs so that premiums can be adjusted upward as necessary.

Deficit Spending

When spending is greater than income, the result is called "deficit spending". One must borrow some money to make up the difference. The graph below shows that the federal government spent less than it received during only two out of the past forty years, in fiscal years 1999 and 2000. The government must pay interest on each negative bar on the graph, each and every year after that bar.

The deficit for a particular year is equal to the total amount of money spent that year minus the total money received that year. Only the spending and receipts that are on-budget are used to determine the deficit. Receipts from Social Security payroll taxes greater than outlays to retirees are off-budget and do not contributes to deficit calculations.

Deficit spending can only take place if money is borrowed by the government, which then increases the national debt. Money is borrowed by the government from their own government trust accounts, from the public and from other governments.

Deficit spending that occurs in one year costs interest payments year after year. For example, in 2011, the government had deficit spending equal to 1,702 billion dollars. The interest on borrowed money varies from year to year. In 2012, it was about 3%, so in 2012 the federal government payed approximately 85 billion dollars in interest for that single deficit.

In 2011, the total interest payment on the debt was 322 billion dollars.

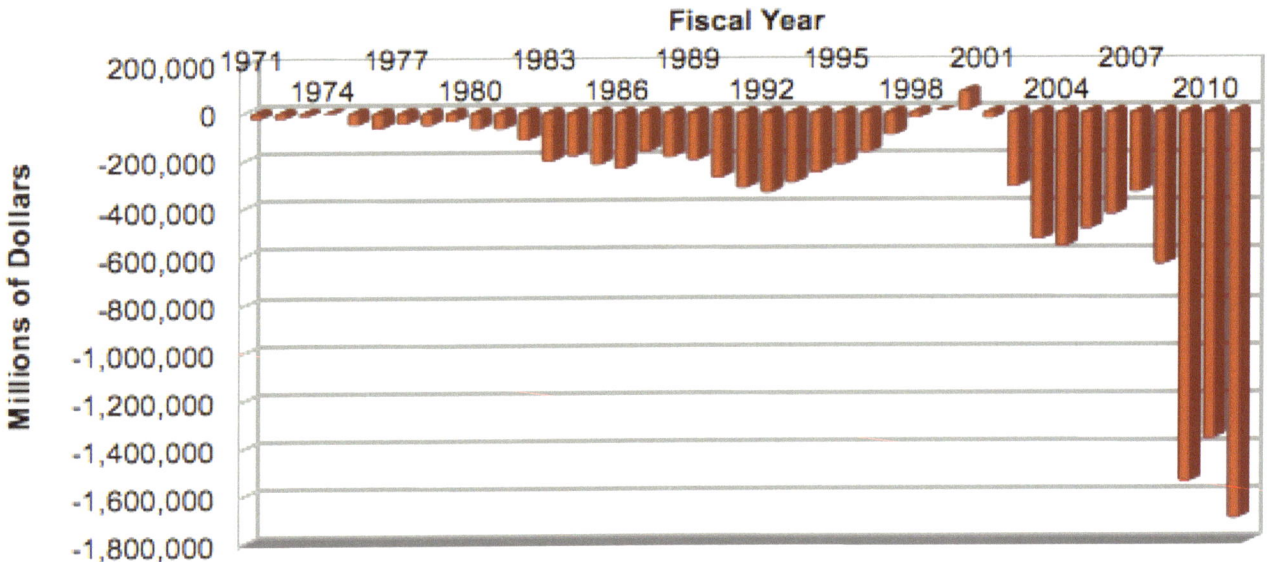

The National Debt

The debts of the U.S. government consist of money that the government owes to the public and money that the government owes to itself. Although the two types are typically combined in discussions of the overall debt, only the money that the government owes to the public has an impact on the economy. When the government borrows from the public, it reduces the amount of resources available in the financial markets for private investment.

In contrast, the money that the government owes to itself has no impact on the markets because it represents debt owed from one Treasury account to another. It will, however, have an impact on the economy when it is necessary to repay these debts.

The portion of the debt that the government owes itself consists largely of IOUs called "federal securities" credited to various trust fund accounts maintained by the Treasury Department. Like federal securities sold to the public, they are legal obligations of the government and are backed by its full faith and credit.

However, unlike federal securities sold to the public, which are assets of the holder, federal securities held by federal trust funds are not assets of the government as a whole.

A member of the public who holds a federal security has a legal claim against the government. In contrast, a federal trust fund holding a federal security is simply the government having a claim against itself. Federal securities pay interest; however, interest from government debt is not usually paid, it is only noted in a bookkeeping account. The amount of the interest owed just increases the government debt.

Money is borrowed from the public to provide **deficit spending;** that is, the difference between money spent by the federal government and money received by the federal government each year. Most of the money owed the public is in the form of marketable government securities. The publics buys treasury bills, notes, bonds and other marketable securities from the U.S. government and this money is used to pay off maturing debt and provide the cash needed for budgeted outlays. Interest must be paid on these securities owned by the public.

During most of American history, the Federal debt was held almost entirely by individuals and institutions within the United States. In the late 1960s, foreign holdings were just over $10 billion, less than 5 percent of the total Federal Debt held by the public.

Foreign holdings of Federal debt began to grow significantly starting in 1970. At the end of 2012, foreign holdings were $5,103 billion, which was 47 percent of the total debt held by the public. The country holding the most Federal debt is China, which held 1,179 billion dollars at the end of March 2012. Japan comes in next with 1,096 billion dollars.

The graph below shows the increase in both public and government owned national debt over the past 40 years. The debt owed the government is shown in blue, and the debt owed the public is shown in red. The flattening out of the public debt from 1998 through 2001 resulted from less deficit spending during these years. Note that the amounts are in *millions of dollars*, so the top value of 18,000,000 is actually eighteen million-million dollars or **eighteen trillion dollars**.

The National Debt

Public Debt in Red; Federal Government Debt in Blue

The public debt in 2011 was 10.8 trillion dollars. Our government paid 322 billion dollars interest, about 3%, with nothing in return; only the privilege to borrow more money.

It is difficult to imagine these numbers. However, this debt is owed by our government. If each of us had to pay off this debt in 2011, every man, woman and child would have paid $34,908.

The figure below shows the history of what has been owed by the public over the last 40 years. The dollar amounts have been corrected for inflation by using FY 2005 constant dollars. The growth you see is real growth.

Public Debt Per Person

in Constant Dollars

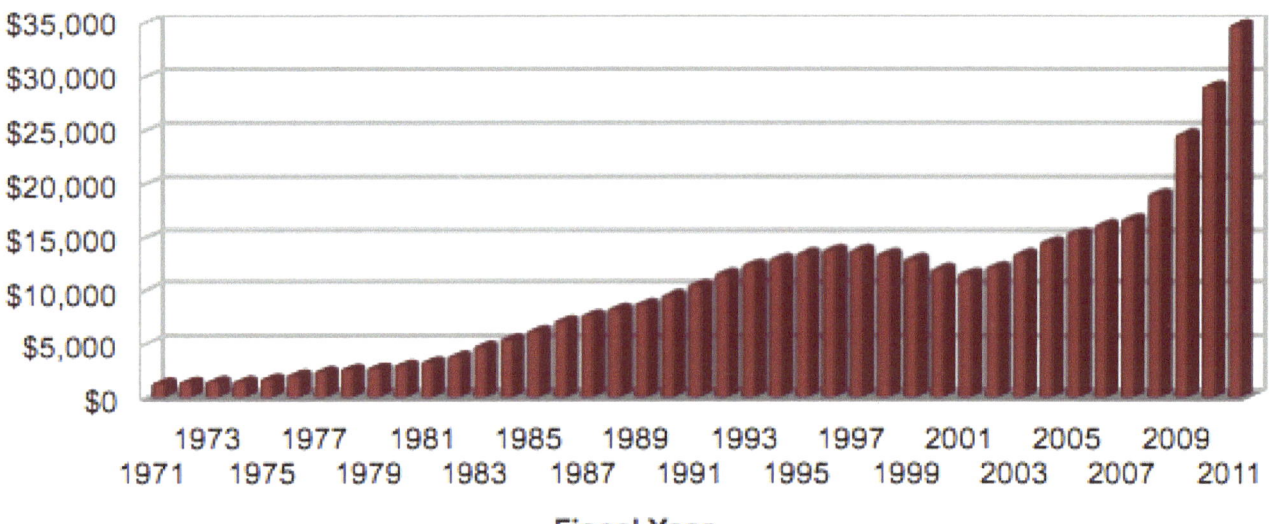

Fiscal Year

CHAPTER FOUR – Historical Insights

Selected Spending Histories

The following pages show spending histories of selected Functions and Subfunctions in our federal government. The graphical information is given as a percent of total spending for each year from 1971 through 2011.

By presenting the spending information this way, we see the areas that we, the people, tend to prioritize. The greater the percentage of total spending, the higher or more important we regard that spending area.

Consider your household budget again. The Bureau of Labor Statistics conducted a survey in 2009 to determine how we, on average, spent our household money. They found the following spending percentages of total income after taxes: We rank housing, transportation and food as the top three. These are our personal spending priorities.

We, the people of the United States, have spending priorities as a nation. Look at the following graphs to determine our priorities as a nation. You can see how they have shifted over the past 40 years.

The functions are listed from highest spending in 2011 to lowest. Notice the scale on the left side of the graph. Some spending areas, Health, are in the five to ten percent range. Some, like Income Security, are greater. Some, like Energy, are much lower.

National Defense

The National Defense function includes the military activities of the Department of Defense (DoD), the nuclear-weapons related activities of the Department of Energy (DoE) and the National Nuclear Security Administration, the national security activities of several other agencies such as the Selective Service Agency, and portions of the activities of the Coast Guard and the Federal Bureau of Investigation. The programs in this function include: the pay and benefits of active, Guard, and reserve military personnel; DoD operations including training, maintenance of equipment, and facilities; health care for military personnel and dependents; procurement of weapons; research and development; construction of military facilities, including housing; research on nuclear weapons; and the cleanup of nuclear weapons production facilities.

FY 2011 Spending

National Defense:	$ Millions
Department of Defense-Military:	
Military Personnel	157,016
Operation and Maintenance	311,881
Procurement	151,938
Research, Development, Test, and Evaluation	80,677
Military Construction	20,908
Family Housing	3,419
Other	13,826
Subtotal, Department of Defense-Military	739,665
Atomic energy defense activities	21,228
Defense-related activities	7,324
Total, National Defense	**768,217**

National Defense

Percent of Total Spending

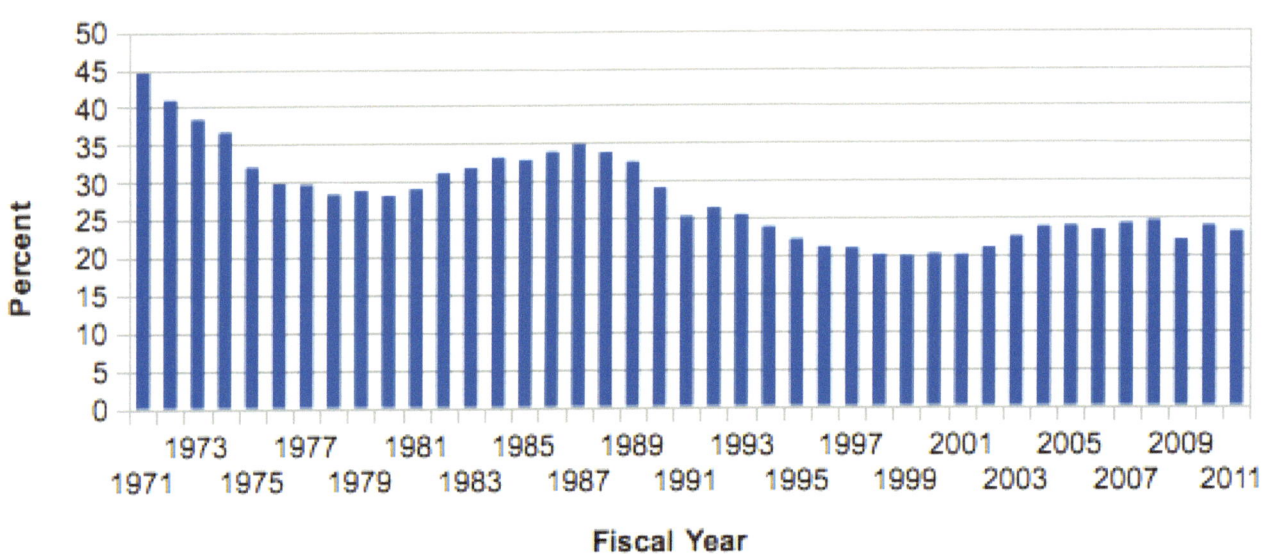

Fiscal Year

Income Security

Income Security consists of a range of income security programs that provide cash or near-cash assistance (e.g., housing, nutrition, and energy assistance) to low-income persons, and benefits to certain retirees, persons with disabilities, and the unemployed. Housing assistance programs account for the largest share of discretionary funding in this function. Major federal entitlement programs in this function include unemployment insurance, trade adjustment assistance income support, food stamps, Temporary Assistance to Needy Families, foster care, and Supplemental Security Income. Federal and other retirement and disability programs comprise approximately one third of the funds in this function.

FY 2011 Spending

Income Security:	$ Millions
General retirement and disability insurance (excluding social security)	7,580
Federal employee retirement and disability	127,066
Unemployment compensation	134,831
Housing assistance	69,367
Food and nutrition assistance	107,219
Other income security	176,591
Total, Income Security	**622,654**

Income Security

Percent of Total Spending

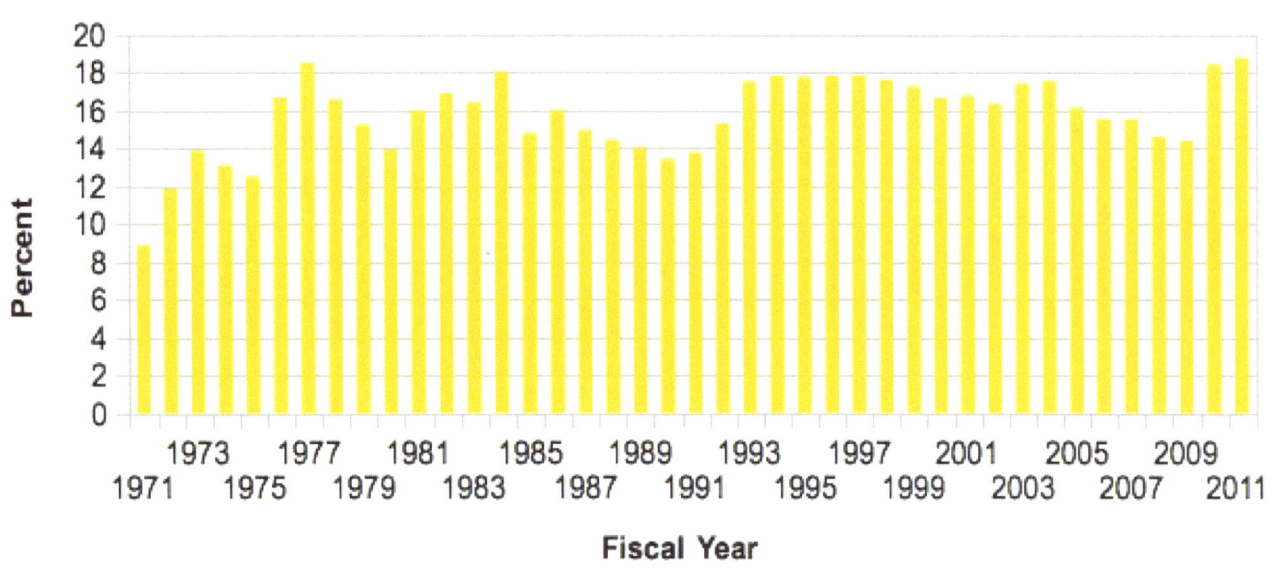

Fiscal Year

Medicare

This function includes only the Medicare program, which provides health insurance to senior citizens and persons with disabilities. Congress provides an annual appropriation for the costs of administering and monitoring the Medicare program. Nearly 99 percent of spending in this function occurs on the mandatory side of the budget, and almost all of the mandatory spending consists of payments for Medicare benefits

FY 2011 Spending

Medicare:	$ Millions
Total Medicare	494,343

Medicare

Percent of Total Spending

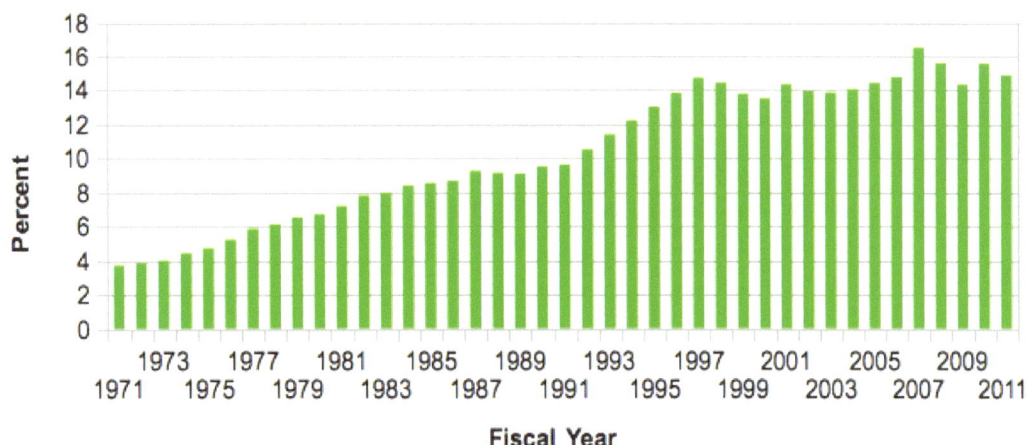

Fiscal Year

Health

Health includes most direct health care services programs. Other health programs in this function fund anti-bioterrorism activities, national biomedical research, protecting the health of the general population and workers in their places of employment, providing health services for under-served populations, and promoting training for the health care workforce. Some of the agencies funded in this function include the National Institutes of Health (NIH), Centers for Disease Control and Prevention, Health Resources and Services Administration, and the Food and Drug Administration. The major mandatory programs in this function are Medicaid, the State Children's Health Insurance Program (SCHIP), federal and retirees' health benefits, and health care for Medicare-eligible military retirees.

FY 2011 Spending

Health:	$ Millions
Health care services	347,043
Health research and training	36,121
Consumer and occupational health and safety	4,453
Total, Health	387,617

Health

Percent of Total Spending

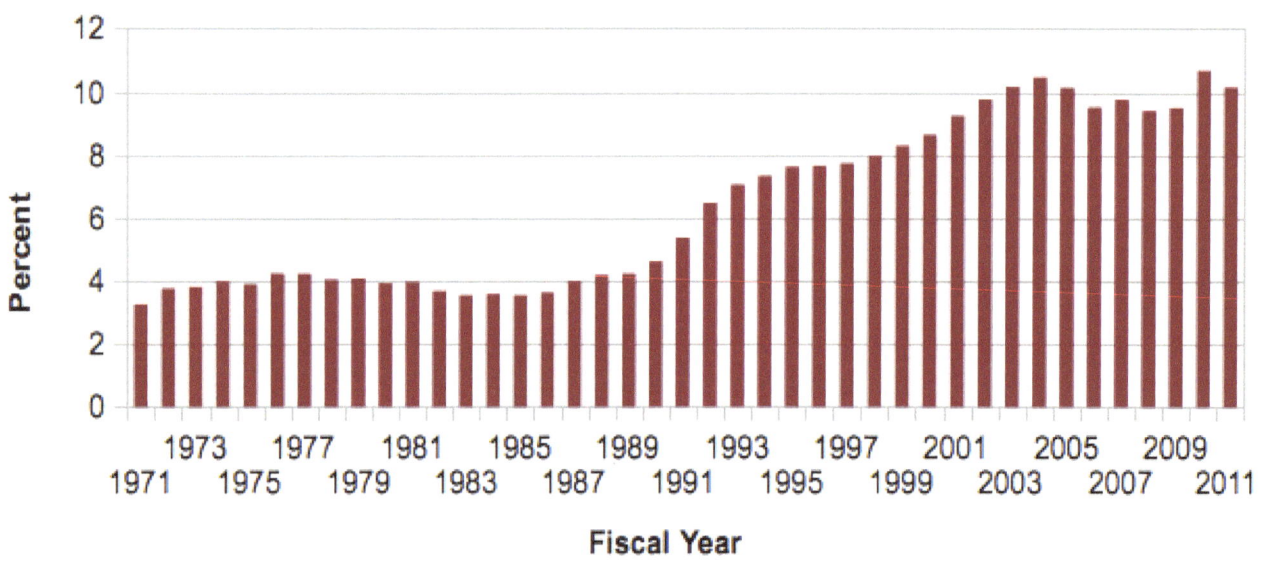

Fiscal Year

Net Interest

Net Interest consists primarily of the interest paid by the federal government to private and foreign government holders of U.S. Treasury securities. This amount is slightly offset by interest income received by the federal government on loans and cash balances and by earnings of the National Railroad Retirement Investment Trust.

FY 2011 Spending

Net Interest:	$ Millions
Interest on Treasury debt securities (gross)	430,414
Interest received by on-budget trust funds	-64,341
Other interest	-42,778
Other investment income	-868
Total, Net Interest	**322,427**

Net Interest

Percent of Total Spending

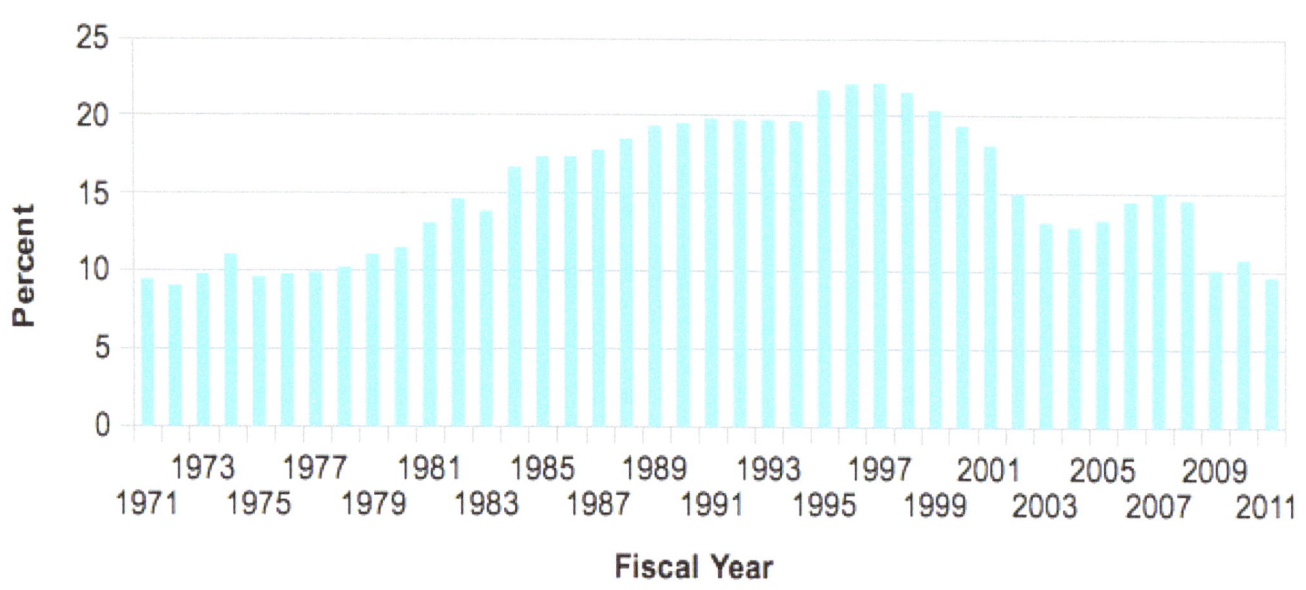

Veteran Benefits and Services

This Function covers the programs of the Department of Veterans Affairs (VA), including veterans' medical care, compensation and pensions, education and rehabilitation benefits, and housing programs. It also includes the Department of Labor's Veterans' Employment and Training Service, the United States Court of Appeals for Veterans Claims, and the American Battle Monuments Commission. Almost 90 percent of appropriated funding in Function 700 goes to veterans' health care.

FY 2011 Spending

Veterans Benefits and Services:	$ Millions
Income security for veterans	72,913
Veterans education, training, and rehabilitation	10,667
Hospital and medical care for veterans	49,627
Veterans housing	1,296
Other veterans benefits and services	6,906
Total, Veterans Benefits and Services	**141,409**

Veteran Benefits & Services

Percent of Total Spending

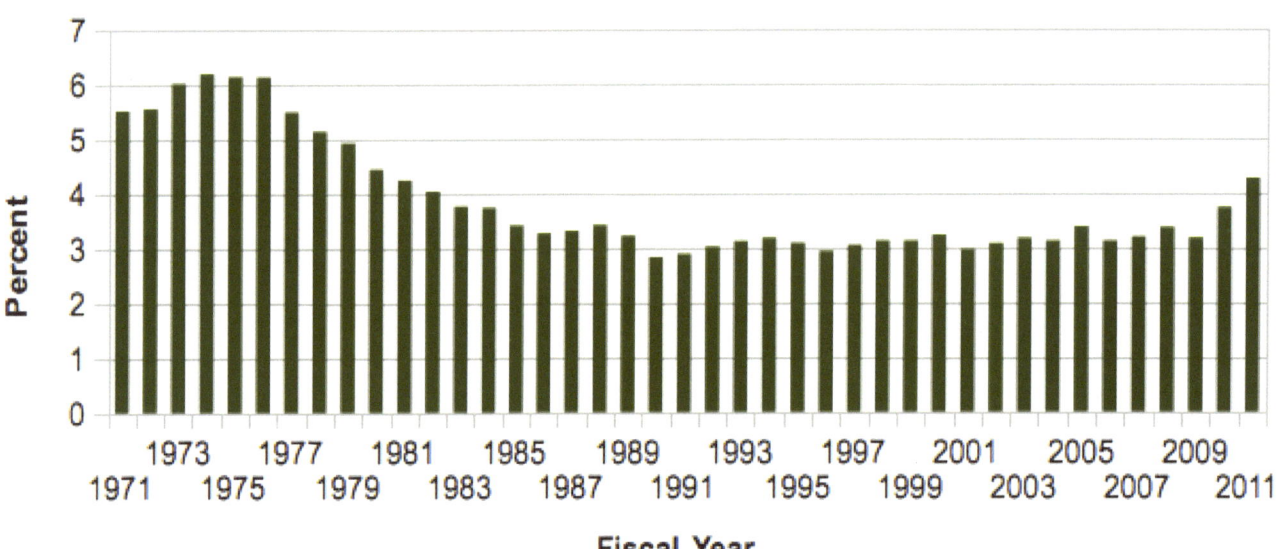

Fiscal Year

Social Security

The Social Security function consists of the two payroll tax-financed programs that are collectively known as Social Security: Old-Age and Survivors Insurance and Disability Insurance (OASDI). This function includes Social Security benefit payments and funds to administer the program. Under provisions of the Congressional Budget Act and the Budget Enforcement Act, Social Security trust funds are off-budget and do not appear in the budget resolution totals. However, a small portion of spending in Function 650 - the general fund transfer of income taxes on Social Security benefits - is considered on-budget and appears in the budget resolution totals.

FY 2011 Spending

Social Security:	$ Millions
Total Social security	117,465

Social Security

Percent of Total Spending

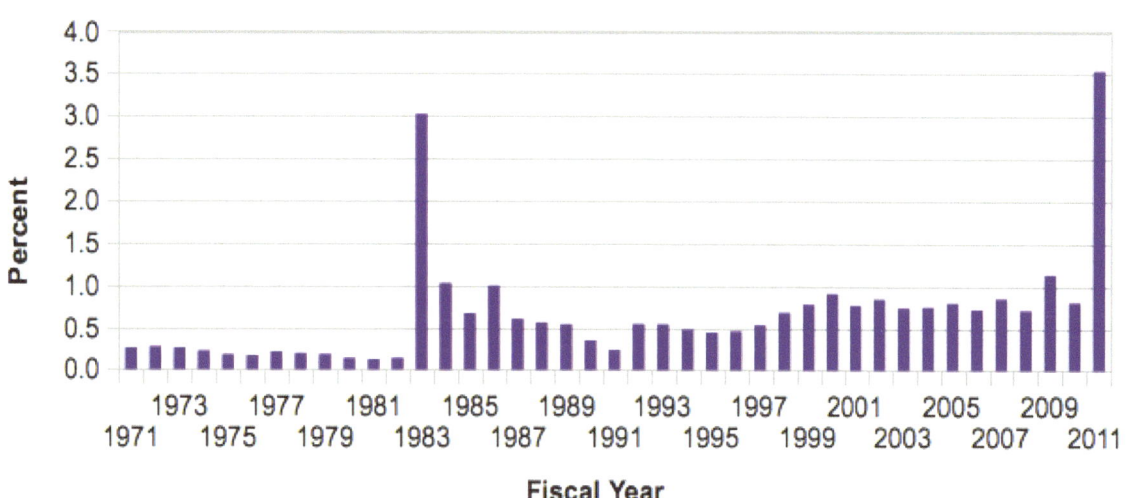

Fiscal Year

Education, Training, Employment and Social Services

This function includes funding for the Department of Education, social services programs within the Department of Health and Human Services, and employment and training programs within the Department of Labor. It also contains funding for the Library of Congress and independent research and art agencies such as the Corporation for Public Broadcasting, the Smithsonian Institution, the National Gallery of Art, the John F. Kennedy Center for the Performing Arts, the National Endowment for the Arts, and the National Endowment for the Humanities.

FY 2011 Spending

Education, Training, Employment, and Social Services:	$ Millions
Elementary, secondary, and vocational education	78,226
Higher education	758
Research and general education aids	3,994
Training and employment	9,074
Other labor services	2,159
Social services	20,907
Total, Education, Training, Employment, and Social Services	**115,118**

Education, Training, Employment, and Social Services

Percent of Total Spending

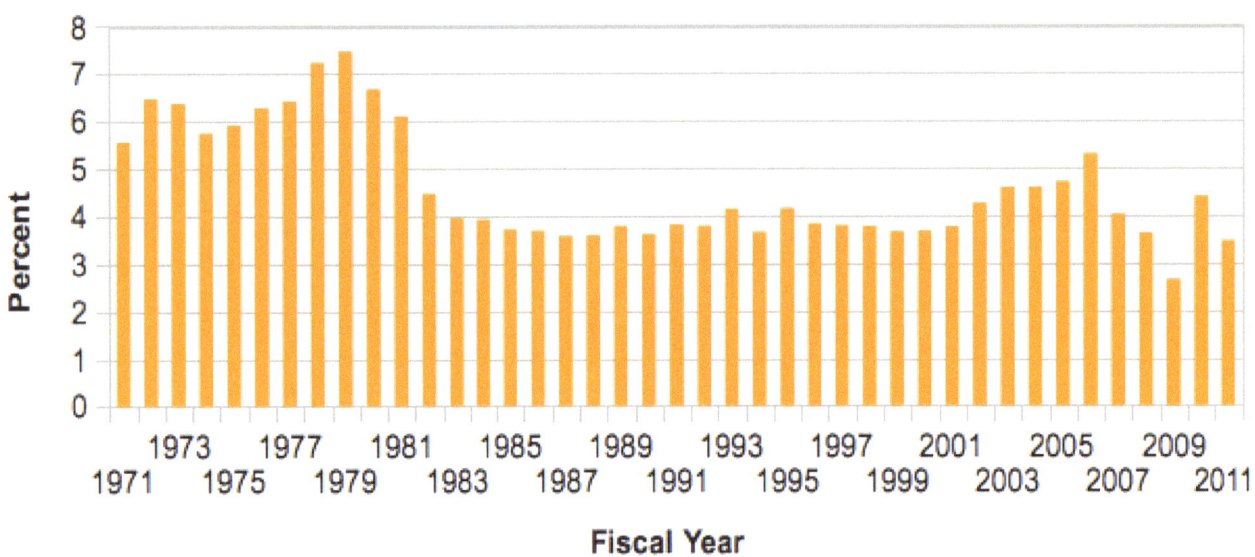

Fiscal Year

Transportation

The function Transportation consists mostly of the programs administered by the Department of Transportation, including programs for highways, mass transit, aviation, and maritime activities. This function also includes two components of the Department of Homeland Security: the Coast Guard and the Transportation Security Administration. In addition, this function includes several small transportation-related agencies and the research program for civilian aviation at the National Aeronautics and Space Administration (NASA).

FY 2011 Spending

Transportation:	$ Millions
Ground transportation	62,020
Air transportation	21,557
Water transportation	10,325
Other transportation	609
Total, Transportation	**94,511**

Transportation

Percent of Total Spending

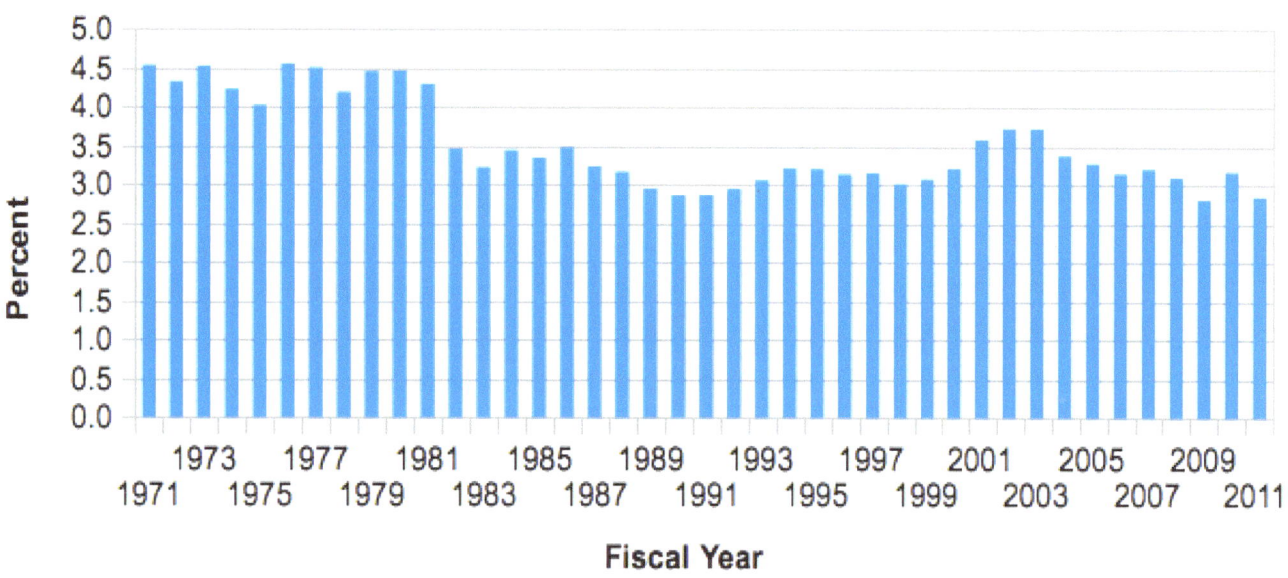

Fiscal Year

Administration of Justice

The Administration of Justice function consists of federal law enforcement programs, litigation and judicial activities, correctional operations, and state and local justice assistance. Agencies within this function include: the Federal Bureau of Investigation; the Drug Enforcement Administration; Border and Transportation Security; the Bureau of Alcohol, Tobacco, Firearms and Explosives; the United States Attorneys; legal divisions within the Department of Justice; the Legal Services Corporation; the federal Judiciary; and the Federal Bureau of Prisons. This function includes several components of the Department of Homeland Security.

FY 2011 Spending

Administration of Justice:	$ Millions
Federal law enforcement activities	31,784
Federal litigative and judicial activities	13,455
Federal correctional activities	7,939
Criminal justice assistance	7,483
Total, Administration of Justice	**60,661**

Administration of Justice

Percent of Total Spending

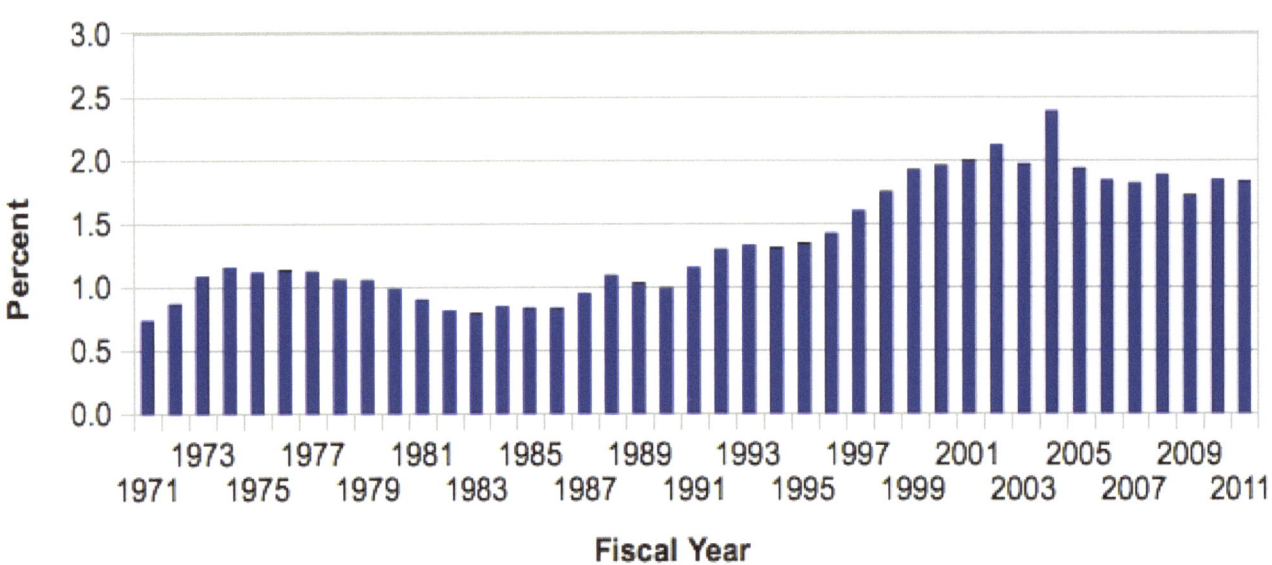

Fiscal Year

International Affairs

International Affairs contains funding for all U.S. international activities, including: operating U.S. embassies and consulates throughout the world; providing military assistance to allies; aiding developing nations; dispensing economic assistance to fledgling democracies; promoting U.S. exports abroad; making U.S. payments to international organizations; and contributing to international peacekeeping efforts. Funding for all of these activities constitutes about one percent of the federal budget. The major agencies in this function include the Departments of Agriculture, State, and the Treasury; the United States Agency for International Development; and the Millennium Challenge Corporation.

FY 2011 Spending

International Affairs:	$ Millions
International development and humanitarian assistance	28,569
International security assistance	11,579
Conduct of foreign affairs	14,983
Foreign information and exchange activities	1,567
International financial programs	-1,526
Total, International Affairs	**55,172**

International Affairs

Percent of Total Spending

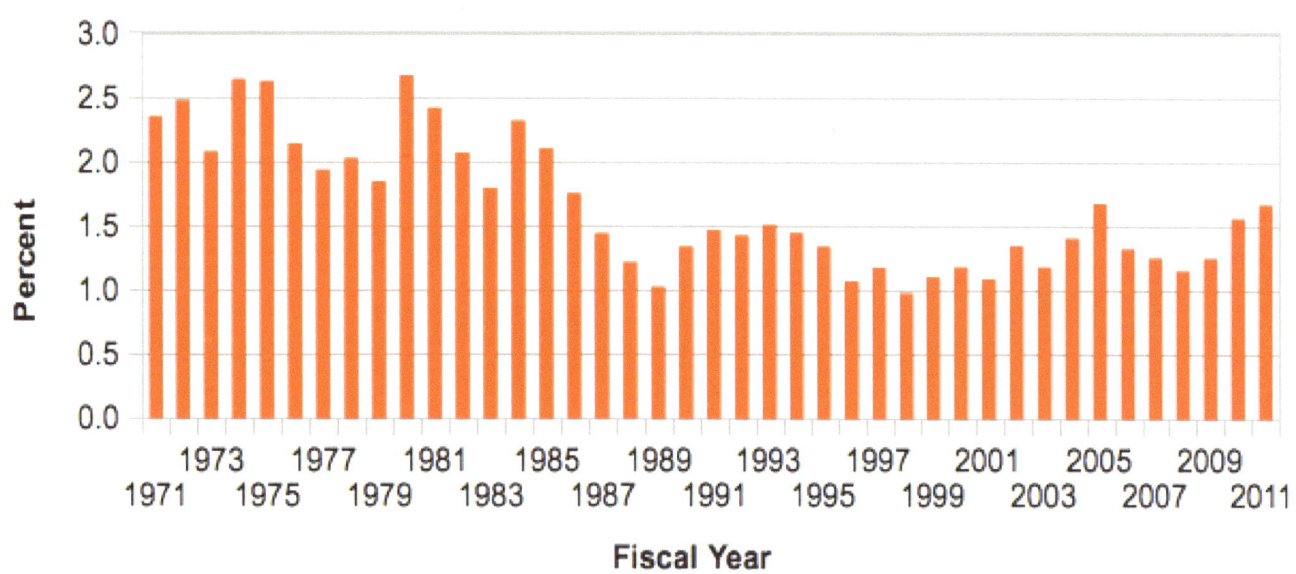

Fiscal Year

Natural Resources and Environment

This function includes programs concerned with environmental protection and enhancement; recreation and wildlife areas; and the development and management of the nation's land, water, and mineral resources. It includes programs within the following federal departments and agencies: Agriculture, Commerce, Interior, Transportation, the Army Corps of Engineers, and the Environmental Protection Agency (EPA).

FY 2011 Spending

Natural Resources and Environment:	$ Millions
Water resources	12,507
Conservation and land management	13,851
Recreational resources	4,053
Pollution control and abatement	10,872
Other natural resources	7,719
Total, Natural Resources and Environment	**49,002**

Natural Resources and Environment

Percent of Total Spending

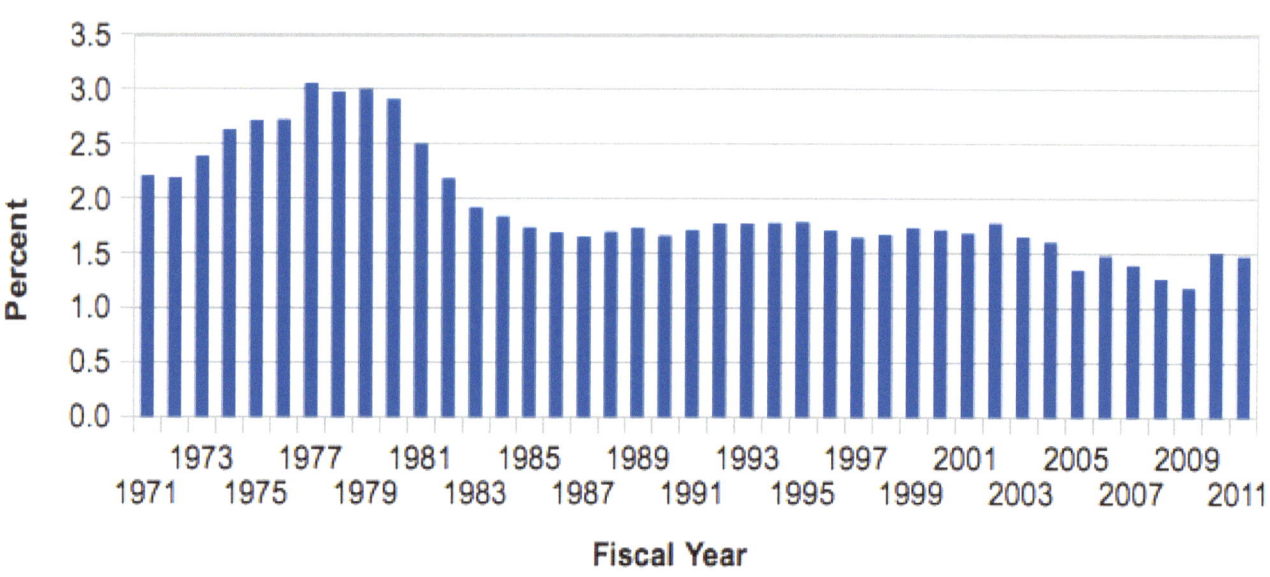

Fiscal Year

General Science, Space and Technology

This function includes the National Science Foundation (NSF), programs at the National Aeronautics and Space Administration except for aviation programs, and general science programs at the Department of Energy (DOE).

FY 2011 Spending

General Science, Space, and Technology:	$ Millions
General science and basic research	14,695
Space flight, research, and supporting activities	18,661
Total, General Science, Space, and Technology	33,356

General Science, Space and Technology

Percent of Total Spending

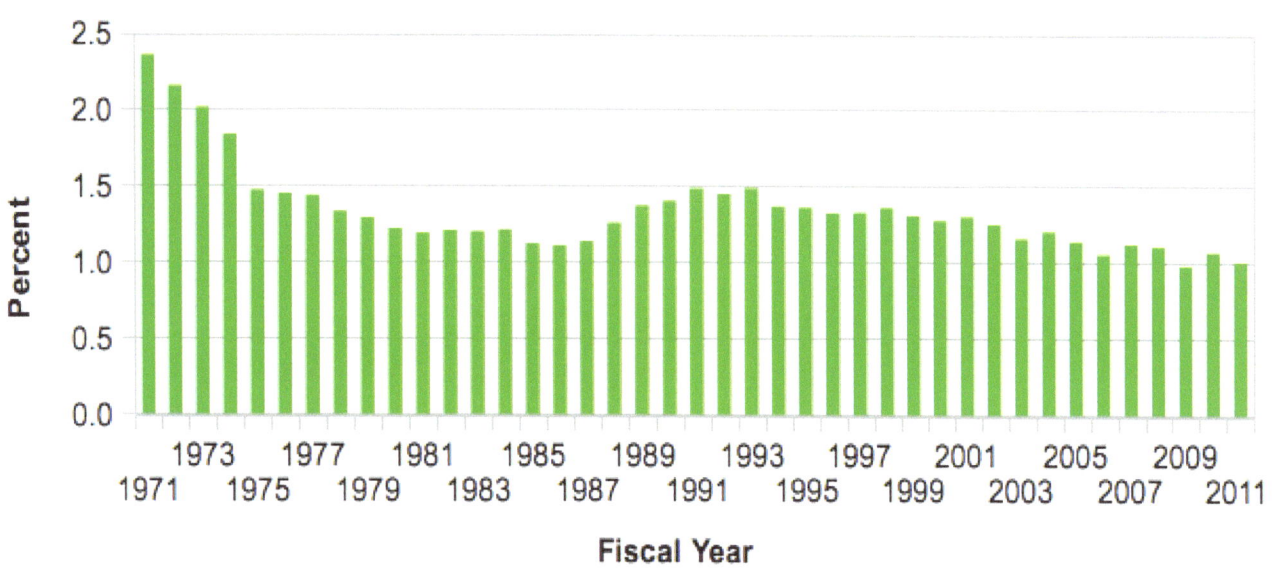

General government

This function includes the activities of the White House and the Executive Office of the President, the legislative branch, and programs designed to carry out the legislative and administrative responsibilities of the federal government, including personnel management, fiscal operations, and property control.

FY 2011 Spending

General Government:	$ Millions
Legislative functions	4,201
Executive direction and management	577
Central fiscal operations	12,196
General property and records management	3,494
Central personnel management	199
General purpose fiscal assistance	7,065
Other general government	5,423
Deductions for offsetting receipts	-1,080
Total, General Government	**32,075**

General Government

Percent of Total Spending

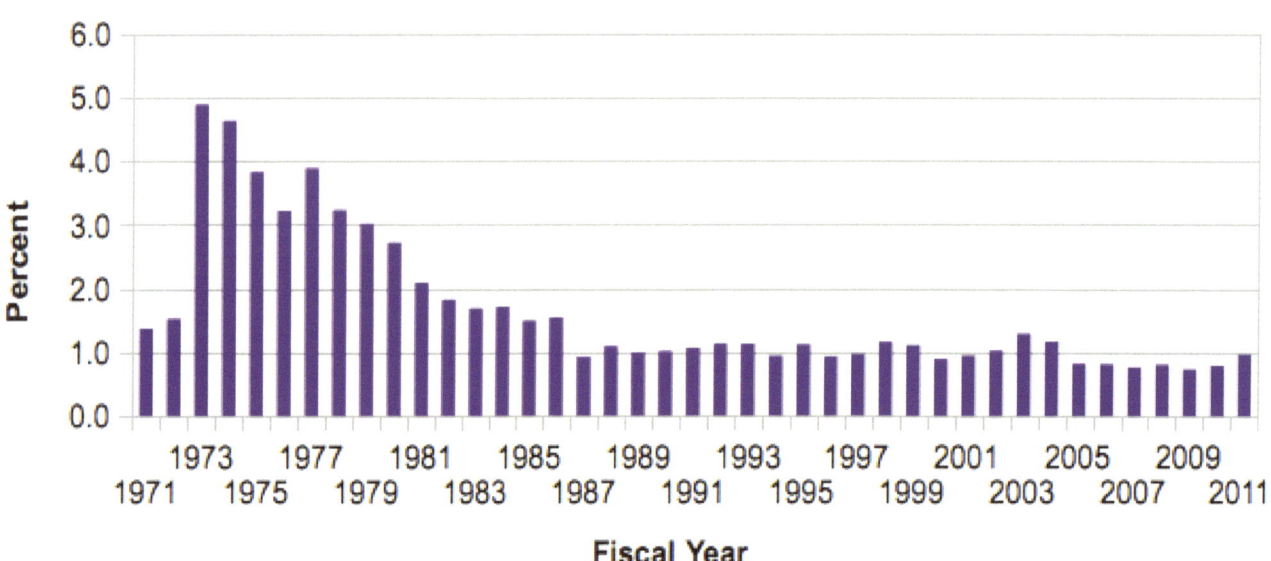

Fiscal Year

Energy

The function Energy contains civilian energy and environmental programs in the Department of Energy (DOE). This function also includes the Rural Utilities Service of the Department of Agriculture, the Tennessee Valley Authority, the Federal Energy Regulatory Commission, and the Nuclear Regulatory Commission. This function does not include DOE's national security activities, which are in Function 050 (National Defense), or its basic research and science activities, which are in Function 250 (General Science, Space and Technology).

FY 2011 Spending

Energy:	$ Millions
Energy supply	13,732
Energy conservation	13,161
Emergency energy preparedness	199
Energy information, policy, and regulation	799
Total, Energy	27,891

Energy

Percent of Total Spending

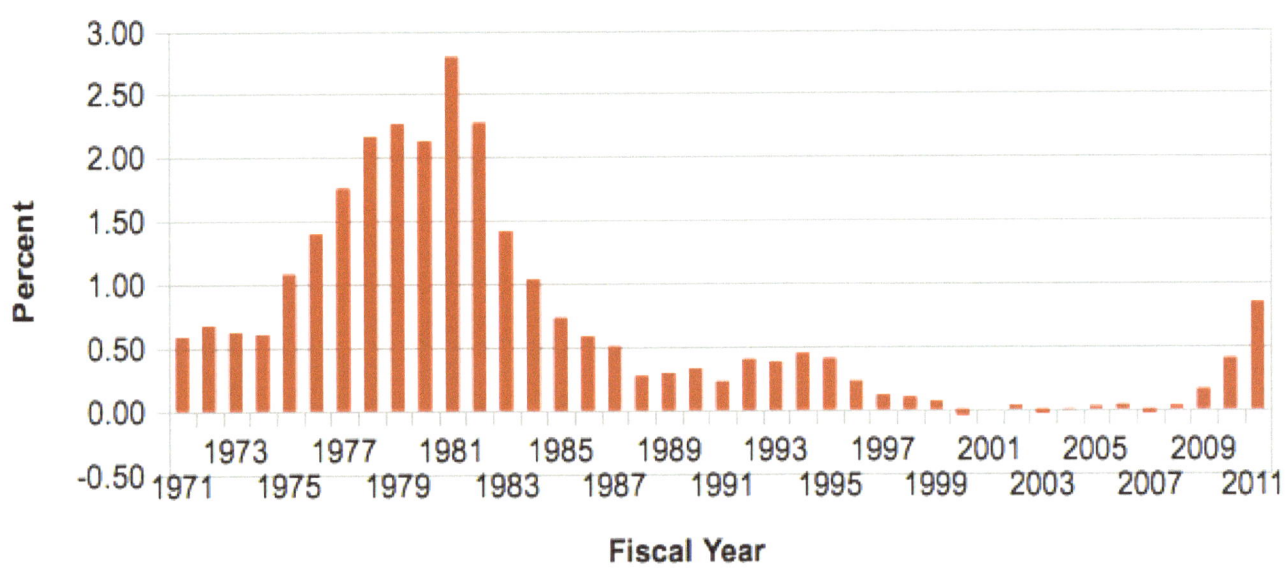

Fiscal Year

Community and Regional Development

This function includes federal programs to improve community economic conditions, promote rural development, and assist in federal preparations for and response to disasters. This function provides appropriated funding for the Community Development Block Grant, Department of Agriculture rural development programs, the Bureau of Indian Affairs, the Federal Emergency Management Agency, and other disaster mitigation and community development-related programs. It also provides mandatory funding for the federal flood insurance program.

FY 2011 Spending

Community and Regional Development:	$ Millions
Community development	11,195
Area and regional development	3,068
Disaster relief and insurance	11,479
Total, Community and Regional Development	25,742

Community & Regional Development

Percent of Total Spending

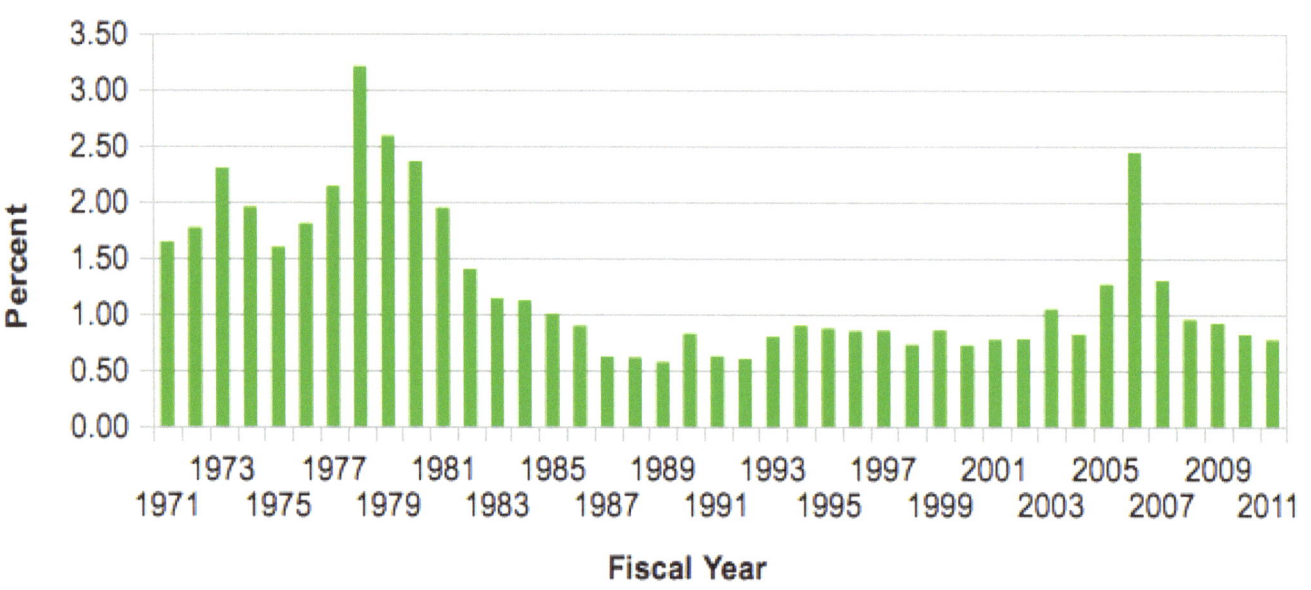

Fiscal Year

Agriculture

Agriculture includes farm income stabilization, agricultural research, and other services administered by the U.S. Department of Agriculture. The discretionary programs include research and education programs, economics and statistics services, administration of the farm support programs, farm loan programs, meat and poultry inspection, and a portion of the Public Law (P.L.) 480 international food aid program. The mandatory programs include commodity programs, crop insurance, and certain farm loans.

FY 2011 Spending

Agriculture:	$ Millions
Farm income stabilization	19,661
Agricultural research and services	5,426
Total, Agriculture	**25,087**

Agriculture

Percent of Total Spending

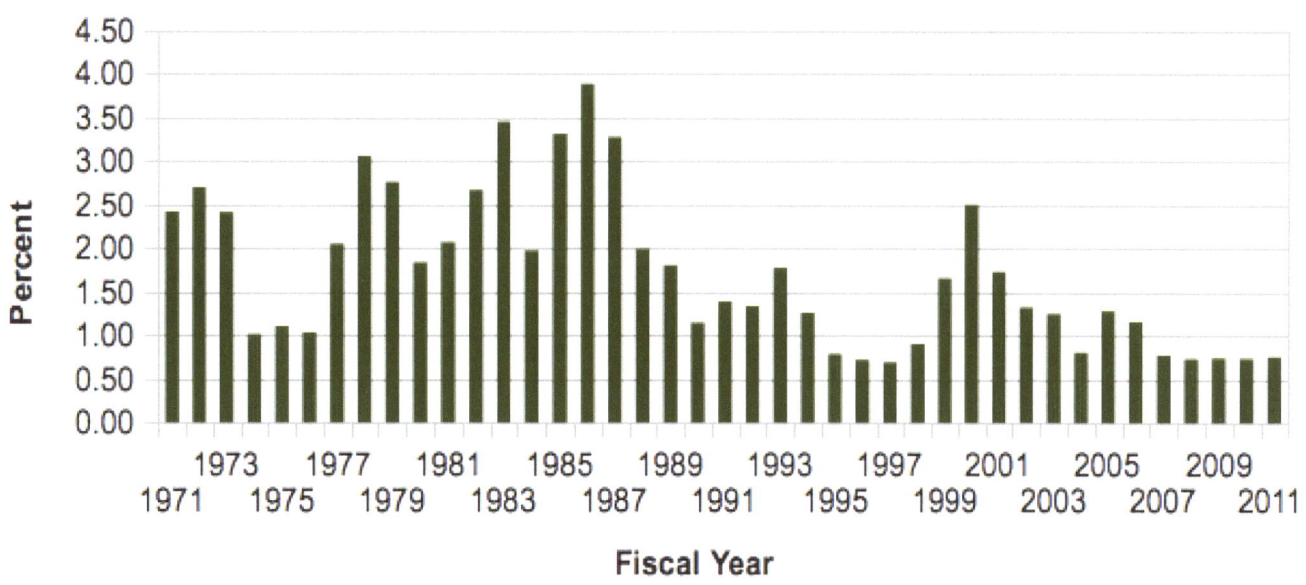

Fiscal Year

Commerce and Housing Credit

This function includes mortgage credit, the Postal Service, deposit insurance, and other advancement of commerce (the majority of the discretionary and mandatory spending in this function). The mortgage credit component includes housing assistance through the Federal Housing Administration, the Federal National Mortgage Association (Fannie Mae), the Federal Home Loan Mortgage Corporation (Freddie Mac), the Government National Mortgage Association (Ginnie Mae), and rural housing programs of the Department of Agriculture. The function also includes net postal service spending and spending for deposit insurance activities of banks, thrifts, and credit unions. Most of the Commerce Department is provided for in this function. Finally, the function also includes funding for independent agencies such as the Securities and Exchange Commission, the Commodity Futures Trading Commission, the Federal Trade Commission, the Federal Communications Commission, and the majority of the Small Business Administration.

FY 2011 Spending

Commerce and Housing Credit:	$ Millions
Mortgage credit	35,456
Postal service	-774
Deposit insurance	-4,123
Other advancement of commerce	-14,660
Total, Commerce and Housing Credit	**15,899**

Commerce & Housing Credit

Percent of Total Spending

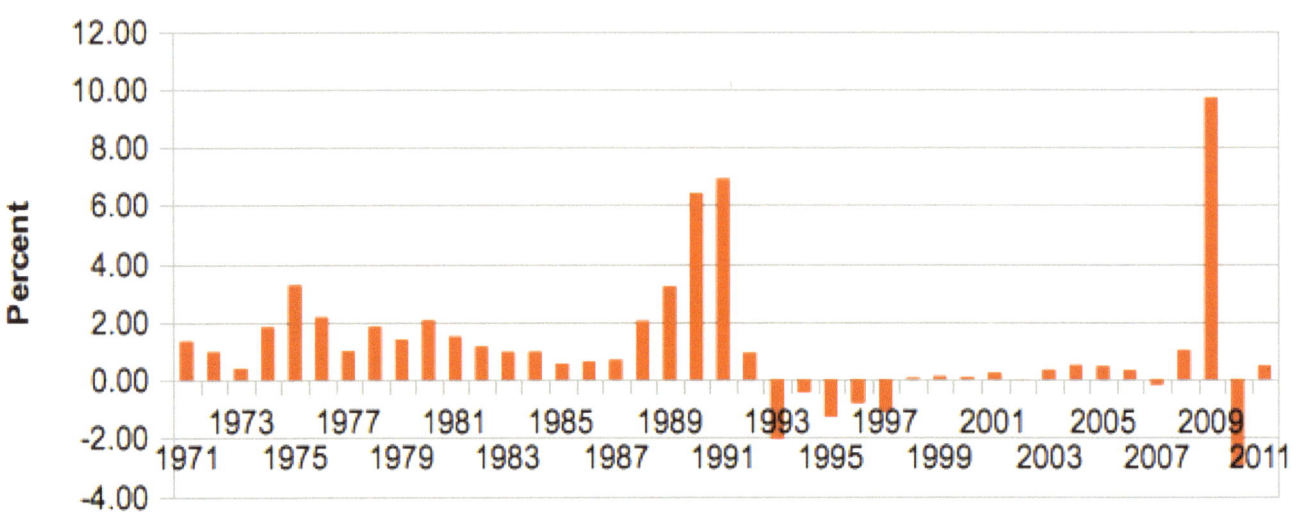

Fiscal Year

So, what does this tell us? Let's talk about that in the last chapter.

CHAPTER FIVE – Responsibility Begins Here

Let's look at Trust Funds

In Section two we learned that Trust Funds are loans to the federal government by the federal government. Interest is accrued which just adds to the tab. So far, we owe ourselves 4.6 trillion dollars, one billion dollars more than our government spent in 2011.

Remember our example of the parents funding their daughter's college using a similar "trust fund"? They borrowed money from their daughters college fund from time to time to buy a boat, take a vacation to Disney World and to remodel the kitchen. When it is time for daughter to go to college, all they had was IOUs in the safety deposit box. What should they do? Perhaps they should fess up to their daughter and tell her what happened to the money they and she had put into the fund. They benefited from it and so did she. They might tell her it was wrong to spend that money and that they apologize. Then they might throw away the IOUs and find a way to pay for her college.

Perhaps that is what we should do with the Trust Funds. We should fess up. We spent that money that was supposed to go for Social Security payments and Medicare payments. We all benefited from it (perhaps) and there is no sense in keeping the charade that we owe ourselves principle and interest. Perhaps we should tear up those federal notes and agree never to have this type of trust fund again. Perhaps we should require that any excess money in a fund be held as actual money in a real trust fund and perhaps we should require that the excess can never exceed twice the past two year outlay from that fund. Then, perhaps, we could go ahead and make the necessary adjustments in the fund taxes so that each year approximately what went out equals what went in. That would reduce the total debt by quite a bit. We then would just have the public debt.

What about the Debt and Deficit?

Let's talk about this public debt? Every time we spend more than we receive, we have a deficit and we have to borrow money from somebody or some government to pay the bills. The public debt is now in excess of 15 trillion dollars!

We pay interest on this debt. For every one-percentage point of interest, we pay 150 billion dollars which is about 4% of the total 2011 federal budget. Notice that in 2011, we spent much less than 4% of total annual spending on many of the function that might be considered important.

What will happen if interest rates go up? For each percentage point up, we will pay another 150 billion dollars for nothing, except the opportunity to borrow more money. And then there is ......

The Budget Control Act of 2011

The "Budget Control Act of 2011" included procedures to raise the debt limit by up to $2.4 trillion, in two installments, with procedures for Congress to disapprove the increases. The Act caps discretionary spending, which, in conjunction with other savings in the bill, saves more than $900 billion over ten years.

The Act required Congress to agree upon deficit reduction of more than $1.2 trillion, and, if no agreement was reached, a second debt ceiling increase of $1.2 trillion would go into effect, accompanied by a "budget sequester".

A budget sequester is when money that would otherwise be spent under current law is held back and is used instead for deficit reduction. Because the Joint Select Committee on Deficit Reduction did not report and Congress did not enact legislation that reduced the deficit by more than $1.2 trillion, as required by the Act, the deficit reduction sequester will begin in January 2, 2013.

The deficit reduction sequester was designed to achieve savings of $1.2 trillion through 2021.

For 2013, that comes out to be a $55 billion cut in defense and a $55 billion cut in non-defense spending. Based on the calculations in the law, spending on government programs will be reduced by $984 billion. The bulk of the sequestration savings come from discretionary programs (those funded by annual appropriations bills) as opposed to mandatory programs.

There is no waiver of the deficit reduction sequester unless there is a declaration of war. The only option for changing it would be to enact legislation to amend the Act.

What is Important to Our Future?

When you consider what we, as a country, need to focus on now, you may suggest the following:

- Educating our children for a more productive, enjoyable life
- Training our workforce in the changing needs of the manufacturing and service industries
- Becoming more energy independent
- Becoming the nation for new ideas, innovations and engineering expertise

If you now glance back at the last section, checkout the function of "Education, Training, Employment and Social Services". Notice that over the past forty years, our spending as a percentage of total annual spending as dropped by one-half, from 7% to 3-1/2 %.

Now look at the function "Energy". This spending as a percentage of total spending has decreased by a factor of three since its high during the late seventies. Here is where we develop new energy technologies. Here and in the function "General Science, Space and Technology" where there has been a steady decline from over 2% to less than 1%.

How are we going to be a growing, successful nation full of satisfied, happy people when we are de-emphasizing these areas? Why is this happening?

Here is why. Look at the functions "Medicare" and "Health". Growth in Medicare has been over 4-fold, from under 4% to over 15%. Health is similar—growing from 3% to 10%. Since there is only 100% of our budget available, when something goes up, others must go down. These are the problem areas. These need the attention of those who serve us in Washington. Is the problem too big for their minds? No, they could solve the problems.

Are they distracted? Yes, they are.

What You Can Do About the Problems

What you are doing right now is most important. You are seeking information about the federal budget. When you begin to understand, you sense a freedom that enables you to understand more. At some point, you will begin to speak to others from your understanding. You will be able to talk about budget issues with your federal representatives and from these conversations, you will see how to act. Most things in our lives follow this pattern. We begin with understanding and end with committed actions.

You will decide exactly what those actions are. You may decide to learn about your government representatives, how they voted and what they believe. You may decide to help a particular person become elected and represent you. You may decide to become politically active yourself. There may be an area or issue about which you feel strongly and you may become active in that area or issue. You may run for a political office. What you will be doing is becoming responsible for your government and for the future of your children and grandchildren.

There are those who say it is too difficult to understand the federal budget or other government issues. They say that we have representatives whom we elected, and they know what they are doing. They say that they don't have time to learn about these issues; they have a family to support and a life to live. This conversation disempowers them and those who listen.

Certainly, our representatives must be intelligent and able to learn how our government operates. However, it is not too complicated for the average citizen who is interested and willing to spend some time to learn.

Many of our representatives had very little previous training in the political system. Some have come from local government but many have not. We have had very responsible representatives who were previously doctors, engineers, football players, actors and homemakers. You possibly would make a very good representative in the House of Representatives or the Senate, if that is what you are interested in doing.

Here are some facts about our federal government representatives:

FACT	House of Representatives	Senate
Number of members	435	100
Term of Office	2 years	6 years
Annual Salary	$174,000.00	$174,000.00
Health Insurance and Retirement Benefits	Standard Federal Employee Benefits	Standard Federal Employee Benefits
Average Campaign Cost	$1,600,000.00	$15,000,000.00
Average Daily Funds to Raise	$2,200.00	$6,800.00
Average Term in Office	9.3 years	12.8 years

Here's an Idea

Back in 2010, President Obama created a bi-partisan commission to identify "…policies to improve the fiscal situation in the medium term and to achieve fiscal sustainability over the long run." Alan Simpson and Erskine Bowles co-chaired the commission which first met in April, 2010 and released a report in December, 2010. The report fell three votes short of the commission support it needed to forward a far-reaching deficit reduction plan to Congress, with 11 of the 18 members voting to back the proposal. A supermajority of 14 votes was needed to formally endorse the blueprint.

Called "The Moment of Truth" this 65 page document offered cuts in spending and increases in taxes to bring the deficit spending of Congress to an end. In the Preamble to the document they write:

"We do not pretend to have all the answers. We offer our plan as the starting point for a serious national conversation in which every citizen has an interest and all should have a say.

Our leaders have a responsibility to level with Americans about the choices we face, and to enlist the ingenuity and determination of the American people in rising to the challenge.

We believe neither party can fix this problem on its own, and both parties have a responsibility to do their part. The American people are a long way ahead of the political system in recognizing that now is the time to act. We believe that far from penalizing their leaders for making the tough choices, Americans will punish politicians for backing down – and well they should.

In the weeks and months to come, countless advocacy groups and special interests will try mightily through expensive, dramatic, and heart-wrenching media assaults to exempt themselves from shared sacrifice and common purpose. The national interest, not special interests, must prevail. We urge leaders and citizens with principled concerns about any of our recommendations to follow what we call the Becerra Rule: Don't shoot down an idea without offering a better idea in its place.

After all the talk about debt and deficits, it is long past time for America's leaders to put up or shut up. The era of debt denial is over, and there can be no turning back. We sign our names to this plan because we love our children, our grandchildren, and our country too much not to act while we still have the chance to secure a better future for all our fellow citizens." *

Our politicians, for whom we have voted and pay for their salaries and perks, chose to be dysfunctional in solving our problems. It is now up to you and me. There are a multitude of ways you can impact the future. Pick one and run with it. It can be fun! It is said: "If you don't shape the future, the future shapes you." We don't want that, do we?

*The full Bowles-Simpson report is available here: http://www.fiscalcommission.gov/sites/fiscalcommission.gov/files/documents/TheMomentofTruth12_1_2010.pdf

References

Budget Function Descriptions:
http://budget.house.gov/BudgetProcess/BudgetFunctions.htm

Population Data:
http://www.census.gov/compendia/statab/cats/population.html

All Receipt and Outlay Data, Deficit and Debt Data from 2012 Budget, Historical Tables: http://www.gpo.gov/fdsys/browse/collectionGPO.action?collectionCode=BUDGET

Trust Fund Data:
www.census.gov/compendia/statab/2012/tables/12s0476.xls

Medicare Information and History:
www.medicare.gov/Publications/Pubs/pdf/11396.pdf

Social Security Information and History:
www.ssa.gov/oact/COLA/cbb.html

Social Security and Medicare Trust Funds History:
http://www.gpo.gov/fdsys/search/pagedetails.action?granuleId=BUDGET-2010-TAB-13-1&packageId=BUDGET-2010-TAB&fromBrowse=true&bread=true

Congressional Campaign Financing Data:
http://www.census.gov/compendia/statab/2012/tables/12s0426.pdf

Congressional Salaries and Benefits:
http://www.senate.gov/CRSReports/crs-publish.cfm?pid='0E%2C*PL%5B%3D%23P%20%20%0A

Average Congressional Term of Office:
www.senate.gov/reference/resources/pdf/RS22007.pdf

The Budget Control Act:
http://democrats.budget.house.gov/sites/democrats.budget.house.gov/files/08.03.11%20Budget%20Control%20Act%20summary.pdf

Budget Sequester:
http://democrats.budget.house.gov/sites/democrats.budget.house.gov/files/documents/12.13.11%20FAQ%20about%20sequestration.pdf

National Commission on Responsibility and Fiscal Reform:
www.fiscalcommission.gov/